NO ONE SUCCEEDS ALONE

A Memoir of Transformation

Duane,
Enjoy the journey!
May God bless
you in all
your miles in
2007!
Lois

By Lois Tiedemann

This book is dedicated to everyone who took part in my journey. Not only does this include everyone that I wrote about in this book, it also includes all of those that I met even if for just one moment,

season or my lifetime up to this moment in time.

I want to especially acknowledge the following people,

for whom without them, there would be no story to tell.

Thank you to my family and friends that I grew up with and who were a big part of my foundational years up through college. Without your love and support, I would not have been nurtured and experienced as great a life without you.

Thank you to Nicole, my best friend in the whole world. You believed in me and encouraged me more than anyone else I know. Thank you for loving me for me.

Thank you to Renee Cermak and all the gang at PSI Seminars in Phoenix and the world. Your contribution was key in unlocking the key to my future.

Special thanks to PLD Team #20 and PSI Seven Team #433. You know who you are. Words won't express my love and gratitude for your support. Enough said.

Last and most certainly not least.

This book is dedicated to three people who I feel left this earth far too early and through their living and their dying were all different parts of my support system in life that I don't even want to imagine not having experienced you and your families that adopted me into your lives. Your impact still lives on through me and the pages of this book.

Michael Brown, you were the brightest light around our circle of friends and still are shining your light to this day. Thank you for your love.

Tamara Kuhnau, you are and always will be the most beautiful spiritual mentor I could have asked for. Thank you for your spirit.

Joel Sans Souci, you were like a brother in all ways imaginable and always listened to me, made me laugh, made me angry and allowed me to order you around when I was a damsel in distress. Thank you for your support.

NO ONE SUCCEEDS ALONE
A Memoir of Transformation

FOREWARD

No one succeeds alone. That is a lesson that took me a while to learn and fully embrace until recently in my life. It was actually the third and final choice for the title of this book. I believe it to be the best representation of my life's journey and I am excited for you to come along and see the impact those four words have had in my first 27 years. That realization led to transformation in my life.

Webster says the word transform as a verb means "to change markedly the appearance or form of. To change the nature, function, or condition of; convert."

For me that word means something even deeper and more personal. It means the complete change of one's mind, body and spirit. A consciousness shift of sorts. I have always been intrigued by the changes people experience along their life journeys. The following pages are a description of the transformational journey of my own life – more importantly the people along the way that supported me through the most impacting events that molded me, shaped me, from a farm girl from Iowa to a college student to an athlete to a successful entrepreneur and business woman.

I believe it necessary to share that when I started this book, I planned on writing about my triathlon experience - specifically the 2005 Ironman Triathlon journey I had journaled rigorously about and shared with many of my fellow athletes. Ironman Arizona was the best day of my life at that time and an event that defined me. It was an event that inspired many others I knew, people who loved to look at their own lives and then choosing to move forward in their own goals. I was honored to be a part of that. This book actually culminates at that event rather than focuses on it. It was that pivotal event that marked a time of reflection on my triathlon journey that I discovered started a lot further back. It was one of the events that inspired me to write this book.

As I started to share the details of how this sport changed my life, a new idea was born. I realized I had to go back to another time and place, back to when I was a 5-year-old girl growing up on a farm in Iowa. Back to the events that I discovered truly shaped and molded me into the triathlete I would later become. Back to what prepared me for the successes and failures of my adult life. Back to where I found myself, where I found my purpose and passion. Back to when I truly became the person I am today.

As a wise pastor once told me, you have a choice in life when you come to a crossroads, a turning point in your life: you can choose to either *grow through* or to *go through* them. We can live in the moment and treasure our surroundings… or we can just plow through those life-changing events without embracing or even noticing what is going on within and around us. I believe these events don't just happen by accident. These are divine moments where the God of the Universe develops us, prepares us, for the next opportunity that may come our way. Where you see what you are truly made of. To test you to ask for support and stay the lone ranger. Where you take notice of where you are at in life versus just stuffing it down and not reflecting what it might mean for you at that moment. This is where one gets to ask, Do I want to settle with not knowing the reasons why we do the things we do? Or do I get to take a risk and grow, getting to explore and discover my true self? Do I want to let life pass me by and lose sight of our vision or grab the bull by the horns and take on life and pursue our dreams and passions? Do I do things the same way over and over again? Do I turn to support? These turning points are chances to move forward or backward – or, even worse, to stay put in that waiting place I call mediocrity.

I hope that my story will shed light on my "transformation" as well as inspire you to reflect on your own life journey and why you are where you are to today. Or, more importantly, *why* you are *who* you are today. Whether you are a triathlete or an entrepreneur or a kid that grew up in Iowa is immaterial. Your journey is unique to you. This story seeks to prompt all who read it to self-reflect, to seek an inner search and exploration for your own meaning and purpose.

As you read, think about these questions. What drives you? What stops you from moving forward? What things from your past are you holding onto? What are your fears? What are your dreams? Where do you want to go? What do you want to accomplish, something that you, and only you, can accomplish on this earth? What is the legacy you will leave behind? Where are the opportunities and solutions in your life that you may see disguised as problems?

May the journey begin.

TRANSFORMATION

"I am not afraid of storms, for I am learning how to sail my ship"
-Louisa May Alcott
"A journey of a thousand miles begins with a single step"

It is said that life is about the journey, not the destination, for it is in the journey where we find ourselves most of our lives. I have found that to be true and have fully embraced it. If we focus on the destination only, all too often we can get caught in the future or in the past rather than in the now, enjoying the moment. *Being* with the moment. I believe that we can all transform – find change within ourselves that shines on the outside - if we consciously think about it.

When I set out on my triathlon journey several years ago, I had no idea how markedly it would change my life. Tranformation was the last thing on my mind when I signed up for the first of many swim-bike-run events. In fact, and strangely for me, I didn't actually plan on doing a triathlon - it sort of happened by default after many years of being a pure runner. In fact, as I look back on it, I didn't choose triathlon. Triathlon chose me.

I guess to better understand my journey down the triathlon road, I want to delve more deeply into my journey before the days of triathlon - to a place where the transformation truly began in my life, the road that took me to where I am today. To the place where many of you may identify with and gather a sense of when you may have started your own "running" journey of transformation.

GROWING UP IN IOWA

"'Is this heaven?' 'It's Iowa.'"
-1989 movie, *Field of Dreams*

Ever since I was a little kid, I have had a unique curiosity about the journey of life, and that curiosity that allowed me to see the transformation in myself over the years. I think it stemmed from the extreme amount of people watching I did at such a young age. My parents were considerably older when I was born, around 40 years old. They were divorced by the time I was five, so I had a lot of time on my hands - time to tag along with my father around our small Iowa farm, to tool around in my dad's Ford pickup truck back and forth to town three miles away, or to hang out with my brother and his crazy teenage friends when they would babysit me while my dad was working or dating. Even just eavesdropping on all my relatives' interesting conversations got the juices flowing. They always had an opinion or gossip to share, if not some sage wisdom! Sometimes I wished I had been born a few years earlier, just to get in on all their journeys! Some of their experiences had me chuckling or even rolling with tears. Others had me wishing to God that I would NOT turn out like them in their stubborn, hard-headed ways. Surely I did not yet know that saying: "What you resist, persists." I am just as hard-headed and stubborn as the next

German. Add to that the red hair, and watch out! "Control that Tiedemann temper" was often heard around the house. I look back now and call that a passion that derived from the heritage of my family and the color of our hair. Made for a beautiful combination.

My love for athletics began at an early age. What made me, the youngest of four hard-working farm kids, drool at the thought of competitive, adrenaline-rush sports? I have to thank my older brother, Rich, for brainwashing me at a young age. He was almost eight years older, and I silently worshipped the ground he walked on. He was a huge Dallas Cowboys fan, loved Charles Barkley and the National Basketball Association and watched as much of the pros on television as was possible without cable. I was hooked - a sports addiction coupled with a competitive drive and a tomboy spirit.

Because of the farm life, none of the older kids in my family – all older than I -really had a fair crack at the year-round sport seasons on which small towns thrive. They had responsibilities on the farm - chores. Chores were of the mixed bag variety. Everything from driving the tractors and baling hay; milking cows twice a day; planting in the spring; harvesting in the fall; feeding cattle, sheep, pigs; or even the really opportune stuff, such as castrating pigs, dehorning cattle or butchering geese, there was much excitement to experience in the great outdoors of the farm. It often meant donning an old pair of jeans, a stained, ratty shirt, pair of oversized gloves, preferably leather, rubber boots to avoid the animal shit (a.k.a. manure) and pulling the hair back in a pony tail or stuffed in a cap. The chore clothes were kept down in the damp, cool basement , our changing room, where the cow barn perfume could permeate and stay clear of the kitchen at any meal time. "Don't you dare go into the house with those clothes!" was the general warning. "Those belong in the basement!"

Before my dad remarried when I was 10, my siblings even had to pick up the slack in raising me as well. I was the fortunate kid, the one that got to start young in sports and who flourished fast. Watching my brother throw the football around, playing ball for blood with all my older and bigger cousins, and having a lot of sports-crazed friends, I easily fell into "jock" status by the fifth grade.

Growing up in the basketball-frenzied state of Iowa, where many youngsters can be found where the game is: on the sidelines as a spectator of a small-town state- championship hopeful; riding the pine for the local dream team; or better yet, hold one of those five coveted starting spots. It was this team sport that first defined my individual journey of blood, sweat and tears, pushing my body to achieve dreams I had been dreaming about since I was born, it seemed. Running as a sport didn't even enter my mind until after the last whistle blew of my high school basketball career. At least not the physical sense of running.

I remember sprinting down the dirt-and-gravel mixed driveway of my dad's farm every Saturday morning in junior high and high school, anxiously anticipating the lunchtime (well we called it 'dinner') arrival of the Northwest Iowa Review, the paper with the best sports coverage of our area. The award they won and the expense they put into printing color photos proved to me that they took pride in their coverage. That same pride filled me as I cut out photos and articles for my scrap books. All the local teams and conferences were covered, and every page was packed – pictures of my role models, quotes from the coach's post-game interview and the current standings for whatever sports were in season.

In my high-school class of 46, most students lived and breathed sports or music, or both. The rest kept themselves busy working on the farm or at other jobs. There wasn't much else to do in our farming community of roughly 1700 people. Everything was closed on Sundays, except for the several local churches where you made darn sure you were in attendance if you didn't want to be the local gossip the next morning. You kept quiet and did not say much if one of your family members missed. Judgment came quickly in small towns and excuses were not tolerated.

Far removed from typical types of entertainment, we grew up respecting the hard-working farmer. My dad's work ethic, sun-up to sundown, was normal for any farmer who needed to provide for their family or simply didn't have the education or the desire to do anything other than what their daddy did. Mothers were hard-working homemakers, bookkeepers, teachers, secretaries, or waitresses, with very few "career" women thrown in the mix. At the time, I took for granted the sacrifices my parents made for me in raising a family on such means, but today I see it differently. I respect and admire all that my parents did. It fostered in me the attributes of discipline, structure and a drive that would set for me a firm foundation for my whole life. I would not have understood my transformation of mind, body and spirit nearly as well if it hadn't been for the solid upbringing they gave me.

By the time I was one of the starting five (we had played six-on-six through junior high) on the varsity basketball team, I did nothing but dream about going to college on a basketball scholarship. My idea of running was the "suicides" we ran during practice – up and down, up and down the courts, tasting blood and seeing stars at the end, pleading with the coach to make this one our last of the day. This was long before my distance-running days began. I could only shake my head at anyone who would dare run longer than one lap around our track. I only went out for track to "stay in conditioned shape" for my favorite season and first love, basketball. This first love, as many that would come after, set the stage for the next part of my amazing journey.

DIVINE MOMENTS

"Teachers open the door.
You enter by yourself."
-Chinese Proverb

As a junior, I started asking my mentor and coach, John Olson, about securing some type of college scholarship to play ball. I had aspirations of great things in my basketball future and I knew I would need all the financial help I could get to increase my chances of going to a good school. I figured basketball could be one sure ticket in getting there. My father was not able to help with any financial assistance in paying for my continued education. I was jealous of my friends that had their parents help them beyond the age of 18 with any money of sorts to go toward education, cars, gas, food, and basic needs and bills. Yet taking on that responsibility at the young adult age I did was probably one of the best things that ever happened to me. My dream of playing college sports was far too passionately ingrained in me that I would stop at nothing to get there. If I didn't have the money to do it and didn't want to have enormous debt upon graduating with student loans, I knew I had to find the way. The solutions that would come through the resources around me at that time still amaze me and remind me of the amazing providence of God.

After much persisting into my senior year, Mr. Olson took me seriously enough to have me talk to the admissions representative of Waldorf College, Susan Fitzgerald, who was visiting my school. Susan told me that Waldorf was a small private Lutheran school, primarily a junior college, located in a farming community not even 3 hours drive from my parents' farm. Mr. Olson had attended the college and knew the basketball coach. He agreed to drive me through a winter storm in north-central Iowa to stay with one of his college buddies the night before they happened to have a scholarship day one snowy day in late January of 1996. That weekend changed my life. Little did Mr. O (as his players lovingly called him) know that his commitment would play a huge hand in my future.

As you go through life you can probably point to different events and just know that you were guided by angels in the shape of friends or acquaintances. After time has passed, you can go back and see that if it hadn't for them pointing you in a certain direction at that moment in time, you may have gone in an entirely different direction. I like to call these "divine moments", when God uses people or events in our life to create the opportunities that are there for us, and only us.

I don't know any other person, my parents included, who would have done for me what Mr. Olson did that weekend. Even to this day he does not take credit for his act of kindness. Not only did he take time out from his basketball season and his life, he also took me, an above-average but not yet Division I-caliber player over icy and snowy roads to a not-so-inexpensive school so that I could land an athletic scholarship. I met the basketball coaches, participated in interviews and essay-writing and secured a (nearly) full ride to Waldorf. Had Mr. Olson not gone the distance for me that weekend, I would not have attended Waldorf College.

That school choice was one of the best decisions of my life. By that time, I had decided I wanted to be an ESPN sports reporter, and Waldorf's communications department had its own radio station and high-end technology to ensure me a great education. Not only that, they had an honors program with opportunities for world travel, an Oxford exchange program and an accelerated three-year bachelor of art's program in my degree – all that, and I wouldn't have to wait four years! It was perfect for this fast-track adrenaline junkie. The 600-student campus covered an entire block and featured a fair-sized gymnasium for the basketball community. The town, Forest City, had a $2 a show movie theatre and 50 cent popcorn. I was amazed that the population was just shy of 6,000! I thought this was the big-time city, a thriving metropolis in comparison to my own home town.

Heading back home that weekend, I could not stop smiling. I did not yet know about the scholarship home run I had just slammed for myself, and already I felt that this was the place I would spend my next three years. Despite the winter blizzard, the warmth and friendliness of the campus and the strong sensation in my gut told me one thing. I had found my future. Little did I know that those would be the next three years of my already on-going transformation, years that would encapsulate some life-changing events and propel me into my running -and, later, my triathlon - career.

As I returned to my senior year and closed out my last high-school basketball game, I decided to quit the track team to focus on my training program for Waldorf. My new basketball coach, Denny Jerome, had warned me that he would send me a rigorous schedule to follow for the spring and summer months in preparation for joining the team that fall. Another divine moment was being born from yet another teacher/coach in my life without my realizing it.

DISCIPLINE

"We are what we repeatedly do. Excellence is therefore not an act, but a habit."

- Aristotle

As you may recall, I had never been much of a runner. My idea of running was to the fridge to get something to eat, as they say. In fact, when I did set foot on the track of my high school, I felt inferior and unworthy of even being there. To me, the hurdle and sprint events were my adrenaline rush, and anything over 200 meters was a bit of a gamble. Anything above that distance and my response would be, "You've got to be kidding me!" I did get stuck in the 400-meter hurdle events from time to time because of the lack of specialists. It was funny, I thought. I definitely didn't specialize in that event, but when I did compete I would usually win a ribbon because so few attempted the event due to its difficulty.

That realization changed me because it showed me that if I put effort into something difficult and stepped forward – ignoring my own fear and others' fear and lack of desire, I could accomplish great things. Sometimes I would take that for granted at that young age. However, it did instill in me determination to do things that I had to do at someone else's request even when I didn't particularly want to. I didn't want to participate in the 400-meter hurdles and yet my coach knew that I was capable. By doing what he requested, I subconsciously learned to do things that benefited me even when I didn't want to. I had to do it to support my team. Just as the chores my father asked me to do. Whether or not I wanted to do them, I knew they had to get done. I was learning selflessness and teamwork. In order to make things happen and to complete what needed to in life, we all can choose to step up and get things done as a team. Self leadership is what I was learning. Discipline, ownership, respect and responsibility to self and others. That was a good lesson to learn in high school and would bode well for me years later as a business owner and triathlete.

The foundation that track did form for me was a firm one, although I already knew that distance-running was a great form of conditioning for basketball. My school formed a cross-country team my senior year, but I never even considered abandoning my second-favorite sport, volleyball, for the battering I saw many a runner experience during the fall season. Once my basketball hightops were traded in for low top shoes, I simply laced up my old volleyball shoes and started plodding on the local gym's treadmill after school.

The gym I went to was very small, roughly 1000 square feet, and very lightly attended, quite a contrast from the monolith where I am now a member. Yet it was on the lone treadmill in that meager training room that I began my running journey. I hated it at first because I was indoors on a machine that didn't take me anywhere, yet I learned to do what it took to get through 10, then 20 minutes without stopping. I couldn't explain what drove me. I had the discipline of a marine mixed in with the dedication of an Olympian, all for the love of basketball – to prove myself on the hardwood later that year at Waldorf.

SEASONS OF CHANGE

"The strongest oak tree of the forest is not the one that is protected from the storm and hidden from the sun. It's the one that stands in the open where it is compelled to struggle for its existence against the winds and rains and the scorching sun."

-Napoleon Hill

"You don't have to be great to start, but you do have to start to be great."

-Unknown

As the spring turned into summer and the Northwest Iowa winter snow gave way to damp April showers and sunny May flowers, I transitioned from running indoor on the treadmill and doing sprints in the basketball gymnasium to tracing outdoor miles around our farm section. I hadn't even realized it: the measuring of mileage on the country roads around the farm was a piece of cake, since there is one road every mile. Dirt roads, gravel roads and paved roads, with farms nestled neatly every quarter of a mile or so. Farms filled with big dogs, some behind fences and others not! Oh, the countless four-legged friends I made at every farm!

Now I had the elements to consider. The wind. The rain. The heat. The lack of television and cute young men lifting weights to keep me entertained. I had no idea the shift that was about to happen in me because of this newfound adventure – the ground beneath my feet and the wind in my hair. I would find freedom, and the open road was where my passionate free spirit would flourish.

The first mileage goal I attempted was simple. One mile. Less than the 20-minute goal I had reached on the treadmill, but I didn't want to overdo it the first time. My dad's farm was at the bottom of the hill. The second half would be the easiest part, but the first half was all uphill. Taking it one step at time on the narrow gravel shoulder of the paved road, I stared down most of the way, making sure not to turn my foot on the uneven path. Running against traffic, I figured I didn't have much to worry about. Not having a coach of any sorts and with no resources such as the Internet or Runner's World, I truly drew within myself and had to be my own coach.

I also had to find encouraging moments to keep going, motivating myself to get out and do it. I know I caused my neighbors some concern – they have never seen anyone running just for fun (or for training) down the road toward town. I remember pickup trucks actually stopping alongside me to see if I was okay. "You ain't lost, are ya?" I just grinned at them with my red, sweat-stained face and said I was in no need of a ride or any assistance. Slowly, they would drive away shaking their heads.

Soon I graduated to Coach Jerome's two-mile-a-day schedule. I was happy to finally be able to go farther than a half-mile out and a half-mile back. Now I could have a change of scenery. It was in the early morning that I ran – just after feeding the baby calves and being in the cow barn with my dad. I know he thought I was crazy for running; however, he also appreciated my rising early to get it done. It was our only time to connect during those busy days. Not many words were said – being close to my dad was not something I experienced a lot. But the wee hours of the day provided some of my best memories – running and watching my dad work.

.

Growing up on a farm was a great environment for becoming a morning person. My father awoke every day by 5:30 at the latest to be on time for his milk cows. I truly admired my old man. I once caught him in the early morning at dawn catching a brief moment of rest when I opened the door to our cow barn, his head resting on his hands as he waited for the water to fill the sink to rinse the baby calves' milk bottles. No one worked harder than that man.

Each morning the cows were milked around 6 a.m., and they had to be milked roughly 12 hours later, 365 days a year, no matter what. It was a system you didn't mess around – otherwise, you had some stubborn and angry cows whose routine had been disturbed.

Funnily enough, I was pretty stubborn about my routine, too. On each and every summer morning, with rarely a day off, I found myself settling into a rhythm of my own. As the months progressed, the days grew shorter, but as I drew closer to the autumn and freshman year in college, my daily mileage increased to three. I had achieved my conditioning goal with some hard work, yet it was curiously easy. I had never seen that dedication in me, or had that much awareness of it, and I was renewed in my excitement for college and all the unknowns it had to offer. I now had a pure addiction.

COLLEGE YEARS BEGIN

"Twenty years from now you will be more disappointed by the things that you didn't do than by the ones you did do. So throw off the bowlines. Sail away from the safe harbour. Catch the trade winds in your sails. Explore. Dream. Discover."

-Mark Twain

There is no coincidence that the ceremony from which one graduates from in high school is known as a commencement. It means the beginning and end, the transition from the last 13 years to the next part of the journey. Whether continuing your education or going straight into the working world, you can never go back and have life be the same. In my part of Iowa, it was usually the time for planning your wedding and looking forward to marriage and kids.

Leaving for college was only difficult because I was saying goodbye to a boyfriend and an amazing group of friends who were either still in school or going to other colleges closer to home. I knew in my heart I was embarking upon a big change. Yet very rarely in our lives do we recognize the change, or turning point, of potential transformation within that moment. We usually see the change at a much later date, if at all. I can fully see that now, several years later, and it has prepared me for the continued change I now go through. Had I known at that time that being at college was going to be all about transformation, I would not have cried as many tears as I left my high-school era behind.

Packed in my small dusty pink 1986 Buick Century with my friends Mike and Angie, my parents followed me as we made the journey to Waldorf. It was a huge benchmark for me. I was leaving the farm house where I had spent my entire life. I was going to be the first child in my family to get a college degree. I was leaving behind the community where my entire extended family lived and where nearly every single person in the town knew me. I had never even flown on a plane before. The only reason I had been outside Iowa, besides one school music trip, was because we lived an hour's drive (or less) from three other states. I had not yet experienced Internet access, and the only person I knew with a cell phone was my brother-in-law, who had a trucking dispatching business and his business depended on his availability at all hours, anywhere. I had lived a fairly sheltered life and now was embarking upon the biggest years of my transformation journey.

Only when my parents and Mike and Angie left me in Forest City did it sink in that I was now officially on my own – an 18-year-old who had left the nest to fly on her own wings into the future. Finally, the day had come when all my expenses from then on would be up to me, and would become one thing I became quite proud of. I had to be self-sufficient at a younger age than many college kids I gained responsibility much earlier than did many of my classmates and respected the value of a dollar.

College dorm life was a fairly easy transition. I lived in Jacob Tanner Hall, a co-ed three-story building that housed men on the north side and women on the south, with a TV room and a hall director's living quarters separating the two. It was an all brick structure that must have been built in the 70s, give or take a decade. It definitely was not new and its interior reflected that. The hallways had mysterious smells that I could not quite place the odor from anything in particular. The rooms were roughly 12 x 12 feet with linoleum flooring that definitely could have been replaced at anytime. Bunk beds and rooming with strangers reminded me of my church camp days; communal showers and toilets were not much different than conditions with my teammates during high-school sports. My new roommate for the next two years, Brooke Helgevold, was also a farm girl from Iowa. She an artist, I the athlete. It turned out we both were Superman fans, of the "Lois & Clark: The New Adventures of Superman" era. We collected pictures of the show off of the Internet, our newest addiction since we did not have that luxury in high school, and created a collage to put on our room door.

I definitely was not one of those anti-social types and meeting new people from all over the world was exciting. I had no idea what a melting pot college could be. Waldorf had a program for

International students, so I made friends from Europe, Africa, Asia and even other stretches of the globe. My eyes were opened for the first time in experiencing other cultures through their own eyes of discovering the United States and I began to realize how sheltered a life I had lived up to that point.

I hungrily dove into classes. As was typical for me, I wanted to prove myself in a big way. I had been a straight-A student, nearly 4.0, in high school and didn't want that to change at college. If I was not running, attending meetings or planning something, I had my nose in a book, determined to maintain my streak of good grades.

I look back now and have realized that I was the epitome of the type-A personality – very outgoing and super-friendly to everyone I met. I was a joiner and, besides basketball, I also joined the student activities group, Bible study groups, FCA (Fellowship of Christian Athletes) and a plethora of other organizations. Waldorf truly fed my hunger for activity and busyness that I had grown accustomed to as a child.

The basketball team began practicing once we got through freshman orientation and the first few days of class. I was amazed at the size of some of my teammates – these women were seriously strong and tall! Since Waldorf was a junior college, I understood that the team was not as hard core as a Division One school;

however, by the looks of these girls, I felt I was a tad bit out of my league.

We all had one thing in common, though: we still had pre-season training and conditioning, with some scrimmaging thrown into the mix, so the coaches could see the new blood and assess how the returning players were showing up after the summer off.

When we ran as a group with the men's basketball squad, I was completely in my element. Being a tomboy as I grew up, I often ran with the boys playing basketball or touch football. So when we combined our group runs with the men's team, it was fun to lead the pack with the guys. We ran down the town streets past the open grassy fields near our college campus, just outside the building which housed our basketball courts and weight room. My hard work of running all summer paid off – hardly any of the other girls, or even the guys, were able to keep a steady pace. I felt like a gazelle, wanting to run even longer than they had planned for that day.

By now running was becoming second nature, very much like a person learning to drive a stick shift becoming accustomed to driving and shifting at the same time. I was on auto pilot. After those first few months, I now no longer felt exhausted from running – rather, I was energized and charged up for the rest of the day. The first mile no longer hurt mentally or physically. It was simply the warm-up.

Running anything beyond that was beginning to come easily.

MY RUNNING PERSONAL GROWTH JOURNEY

"Bid me run and I will strive with things impossible"
-Shakespeare

I want to take this chapter to describe my discoveries I made recently about my running discipline and self-motivated tendencies.

Today, when I look back on that time in my college experience, I realize that by that time in my life I had not yet realized that running on auto pilot really symbolized more than just the physical running part of my life. Today, however, I can see there was a much deeper emotional component. Being on auto pilot, or "emotional running", as I like to call it, was something I had been very, very good at without realizing it. It is what happens when I was going at full throttle in life, in most areas, if not all, and I lost sight of who I really was and didn't even know it was happening. I chose to allow the events, choices and even people in my life to override my hearts' desires and I stopped listening to that small, still voice within that I trusted as a kid, that was my true nature, and I started down that path of acceptance of mediocrity and settling for whatever comes my way at the time.

I read in a recent article by Dr. Bruce Gordon, the Senior Advisor to the President of Campus Crusade for Christ, Canada, that emotional running fast becomes an escape, for it means that we do not have the time to focus on those issues which cause pain. We all find ways to "run" away from situations, those life events, that hurt us deeply and shook us to the core of our beings. By never really dealing with those obstacles and painful times, we run from them instead and maintain a busy life, throwing ourselves into anything and everything that keeps us numb. Examples of this are overcommitting ourselves at every opportunity (not knowing when to say no), working overtime, never taking time for ourselves, never going on vacation, not working at all, never volunteering, the list could go on and on. Whether or not those things that we involve ourselves with is something we really want to do or something that is truly a positive focus in which we should be putting our energies toward is a non-issue in our minds. As long as we are keeping busy, that is all that matters. Many times, we find great success, or what we see as fulfillment, in doing these things. We feel we are served well and even can become obsessive or compulsive in our behaviors, most often with prices to pay that effect ourselves, our families and ultimately, the world.

I completely see myself as that person described above and it took a lot of change and transformational growth in my life to recognize it. I believe that running, and later triathlons, was my vehicle that allowed me to channel my emotional energy within the athletic arena that I was experiencing inside of myself. Sports and academic success in college served as my numbing medicine that took me through several years in college and beyond. It was the façade I thought the world wanted to see. Success defined who I was, or so I was led to believe. It was when I truly put on the masks of happiness and told myself and everyone in my life that I was happy with where I was at and excited about what I was becoming. Little did I know that I was actually heading down the path of stifling my true dreams and desires by choosing this route.

The older I get, the more I realize that many times as human beings – and specifically me as the type-A personality I had been nurtured to be – we throw ourselves into the rat race of life at a young age and choose not to question it until a later age.

When I got to college and even afterward, I had some people truly admire my skills to be self-disciplined and independent. I realize now that it mostly stemmed from my childhood and that since my siblings were older and had their own lives to lead, I had time to create for myself great disciplines and structure of my own.

Looking back on my running career up until that point, by age 19, my runs became my daily meditation time, my solace, my escape, my alone time – the time that replaced my independent times as a little girl. Being alone was something I had never really done well since I was a child on the farm. It took me years to realize that after my parents divorced and my mom left, my father spent most of his waking hours working out of the house. It was during those years of my life, ages 5-10, that I developed my creative juices, as well as most importantly, my ability to escape from reality by keeping myself busy. I was able to spend a lot of time alone.

By the second grade, I started taking piano lessons, and the every-day practice time became second nature. It was my first test in applying myself and being good at self-motivation, with the side benefit that I was pretty quick at picking up the music. I found fulfillment in that achievement. I believed I had proved myself by accomplishing something and doing it well. My free time led to the imaginary friends with whom I spent my time during summers so I would not be lonely. I also caught myself up in the lives of people like Laura Ingalls Wilder (the one on television) or characters from other shows that were on after school.

My investigative nature and free spirit of adventure was being born. After a good rain, I enjoyed nothing more than making aluminum-tin mud pies in the grove of trees behind our house. I accumulated many a bump, scrape and scar as I played around on the farm yard and in the fields, exploring every nook and cranny. Later, caught up in the rat race of life, I wondered, "Where has that girl disappeared to?"

Shortly after my dad remarried at age 10, I found activities to fill every hour of every day, activities I thought would push me into having a filled life. Yet it was not as fulfilling as when I carved out that run each and every day. By junior high I was active in volleyball, basketball, track and events throughout the school year. Add to that piano and flute lessons, along with chorus and band contests and concerts – my propensity for filling in those cracks of spare time was an art I discovered I thrived at.

Ironically, later in life I was told by my step-mother that the last name "Tiedemann" had a meaning that definitely defined me. "Keeper of the time" not only fit my father, the diligent, hard-working, schedule filling master, it also described me to a T. I could fit more in 24 hours than God himself, or so it seemed. This helped me fare well as an athlete, a student and a business person. However, I did not fit in much quiet or alone time for myself. I preferred to be kept busy and always on the go. Today I realize that there are prices to be paid for that propensity. It took one hard lesson in my college basketball season to grab my attention and help me learn what that was all about.

PRE-SEASON TRAINING DECISION TIME

"In every adversity there lies the seed of an equivalent advantage. In every defeat is a lesson showing you how to win the victory next time."

~Robert Collier~

As we pursued those first weeks of pre-season training, I quickly developed a love for my team. I could see the true jocks, those of us that loved sweaty, stinky clothes. We lived for the feel of sweat trickling down our backs and on our foreheads because it made us feel as though we were truly giving our all. Throwing our bodies relentlessly into defenders or defending baskets until the end of a scrimmage, just as though it were life and death whether we allowed the other team to score. There were also the naturally beautiful girls who still screamed in horror if they broke their nails or if someone spilled blood on the court.

I was definitely one of the smaller players and had to use my speed and love of running to outplay many of the girls. My forte came at the end of practice when our sweat-stained bodies and red faces took the baseline to start the required daily sprints. Already exhausted from three hours of training, our bruised and tired bodies had to muster up the strength to drag ourselves down the court and back, down and back at our coach's request

This was where I found my body cried out in joy and triumph, noticeably different from my high school days of post-practice running. Back then I saw it as punishment, but not anymore. My already cardio-conditioned body stepped to the line with a light-footedness that could not be matched. Only two other girls on the team could even come close to staying with me in the sprints. They were the point guards and had naturally great speed and agility. Had they worked as hard as I that summer to be in tip-top running shape, I would have had a hard time keeping up.

I felt light when I ran. I felt freedom. I experienced a feverish frenzy, a hunger deep within my blood that drove me to finish first. I already knew after one week that I was quite possibly one of the weakest links on the team, as far as a specialty position or even general basketball skill was concerned. In high school I could play all positions and play them well; however, at the college level, that was not considered a strength, but rather a weakness. Almost every other girl had been recruited for their special skill as a point guard, a shooting guard, a defender, a center, a power forward or a swing man. I knew from the get-go that I was not starting material and would probably not see a huge amount of playing time that year as a freshman. Very humbling, yet at that point I was very receptive to that. I loved my coaches and I loved being part of a team.

I even enjoyed the camaraderie I had developed with the boy's basketball team members and their coach, Mr. Brown, whom I also knew from running class.   Yes, I did find a running class at Waldorf my freshman year. I couldn't believe my fortune – that was the easiest class I ever took! Running laps in the gym was the curriculum, which helped build my love for and efficiency at my newfound love.

My first major hurdle and most difficult "turning-point" decision came early on in my freshman season. After those first three weeks of pre-season training, Coach Jerome and Assistant Coach Steve Hall called me into their office. I did not know exactly why they had called me in; however, I soon found out it was not to be an easy meeting. In fact, it would be a huge teaching moment for me.

As I sat down, I could sense a different vibe in the room. It appeared that both coaches wanted to chat seriously, yet I could not figure out the subject or the reason for talking. Coach Jerome started out by sharing how he felt I had made a great contribution to the team so far and that my running and work ethic were undoubtedly a strength for the team. I nodded eagerly, taking in his praise as a good sign and agreeing that I had worked hard, knowing that it was an honor to be on the team and something I embraced with deep satisfaction.

He then stated something I had not realized, something I had taken for granted because of my small-school background. A couple girls were going to be cut from the team prior to the season, simply because there was no need for all of the girls to be on the team. He had chosen the starters with ease and was now narrowing it down to the bench – those who would stay on the team to support the starting five and those who would have to leave. With a sinking feeling in the pit of my stomach, I immediately realized what was happening.

He didn't have to say anything more. I knew that I was one of the girls he was considering for the last positions. He reassured me that even if I was let go, I would still maintain my small athletic scholarship for my first two years at Waldorf. He wanted to give me the choice of whether to stay on the team, given that I would see little playing time because of my lack of strength in any particular position. Despite my strengths in conditioning and hard work, I could not realistically expect to play much at all given the solid team we had. It was hard to hear, but I appreciated that he truly cared to even give me the choice, something he was not doing for anyone else.

I sat back, a bit dazed. I had never been in this position in my life. I wish I could have seen my face. I had always been one of the first kids picked on the kickball teams in elementary school. I had always been one of the starters of any team sport. I had always been the top musician in my band and in my piano-playing days. I had never even considered the option of NOT being on the team, let alone not seeing any playing time. I could always prove, in whatever arena, that I was worthy of great things, a huge asset to any group. My emotional running had served me very, very well to that point and then backfired at the same time. My drive to achieve greatness in all things, led me not to achieve excellence in any one thing, or in this case, any one position. To me his option of giving me a choice was just like rejection, and I instantly felt that this decision was too much for me to handle. I almost begged him to make it for me. I would rather have him decide than leave it to my own thoughts.

I left his office in a fog. I don't remember much about walking back to my dorm, but I knew instantly that this decision would chart a course for my future. On one hand, I had gone to this college specifically to play ball and if I gave up that opportunity, what would people think? If I had not received that scholarship, would I have considered Waldorf after all? I almost felt as if someone had kicked me in the stomach – as if someone had told me they were going to throw me a birthday party and then, the day before the event, canceled the celebration. What would my season look like as a benchwarmer? I had never been a benchwarmer. Ever. I had often looked with pity upon those that had to "ride the pine". Funnily enough, I had never put myself in their shoes, but now, I was looking at a decision that would put me in exactly that place.

I knew the time commitment to the team was going to be long and demanding. Practicing almost every day, attending games all over Iowa and Minnesota, missing out on classes and campus activities, spending my entire fall/winter months wholly devoted to my teammates – all the while, not really having any personal achievements to show for it. For the first time in my life, I would not be recognized directly as a key part of the team's success. My participation would simply be during practices as the supporter and encourager. The coach had not said that I would never play; however, I received it that way and could only focus on that. Questions filled my head and my heart.

I remember crying lots of tears and asking, Why did this have to happen this way? What was the point? Why did I end up at Waldorf if I wasn't meant to play at all? If I did go through with it, would I be guaranteed a starting position my sophomore year? Or was I simply going to be on the bench forever? Why did the coach even give me the choice? Couldn't he just make the decision so I didn't have to go through the agony?

That situation caused me to stop and reflect for the first time in my fast-paced life. I realized I had a pretty easy life growing up. Even though my parents were divorced at a young age, I really had a life full of love and support, which got me to that crucial moment in my freshman year at Waldorf. Everything I attempted, I achieved.

Everything from sports to music to academics came to me easily. I never gave up on anything I pursued. I did not believe in quitting or throwing in the towel. I had confidence born in me and moved forward in faith, knowing and believing that God was in control and had blessed me with physical and musical talents. I had never really been tested that deeply in emotional decisions in my life. This was the first true matter of the heart, the first tough decision. It was a huge turning point for me.

I sought out support from friends as if it were a life–or-death situation. I truly had a heavy heart and, not ever having lost a close loved one in my life, it felt as though I was experiencing grief and mourning to some degree. I went from class to class in a fog, puffy-eyed – remnants of the tears cried as I tossed and turned through the night. I asked for advice from my sophomore teammates and realized that they truly cared for me because they didn't just tell me what to do. They simply listened and helped me sort out my own answers. I was so used to being told how to choose that this was a different position to be in, but I welcomed it, even though I didn't fully comprehend at the time how new an experience it was. Looking back, that was real love and friendship – supporting me in figuring out my own decision. They knew they couldn't make it for me. What a refreshing change from being told what or how to do something my whole life up until that moment, or not feeling judgment for my decision.

The main thing I would have to face if I stuck with the team was the humbling experience of not playing much during games. I had always been one of the best players on the team. I had always shone brightly and found accomplishment in that. I began to realize that I had gotten used to proving myself through achieving and always being the best in whatever endeavor I pursued. I had found my recognition in winning games, pushing my limits and always being on the front line. My pride had been tarnished and I was faced with a new opportunity. I was choosing in, or choosing out – making a choice with nothing to go on, since I had never been in this position before. My future was in my hands.

After much thought seeking the wise counsel of my friends, I decided to stick it out and stay on the team. I felt that this was what I truly wanted. That was ultimately the transformational point that would propel me into my running career, setting the foundation for the triathlon years later. I had no idea that it was the wisest decision that I could ever have made and that it would be pivotal in defining my future.

PLAYING A SUPPORTING ROLE

Some people have greatness thrust upon them. Few have excellence thrust upon them...They achieve it. They do not achieve it unwittingly by doing what comes naturally and they don't stumble into it in the course of amusing themselves. All excellence involves discipline and tenacity of purpose."

-John William Gardner

One lesson I have learned in my own personal growth journey is this, no one succeeds alone. I had always been self-sufficient in my early years, and I completely missed the concept of supporting others – being that supporting role versus the leader - nor was I open to asking for help for myself. It wasn't until recently I realized that giving and receiving support in our lives is a spiritual journey in and of itself.

When I was younger, I never wanted to appear weak by asking for help, nor did I want to waste much time in giving it. I was a lone ranger with my own goals and my own glory to accomplish. If I helped myself succeed, then others had to do the same. So, during that basketball season of learning how to support the team by encouragement and scrimmaging, I saw a different side of myself as a human being.

As I rode the bus on the long treks to away games, I developed some amazing friendships that endure today. I also learned how to be a supporter, and how a team is only as strong as its weakest link. Even though I sensed I would not be starting material, I realized throughout the season that my hard work and scrappy, fast-paced running game would help my team get to the post-season. I was able to be a leader behind the scenes instead of in the front lines.

My fire for running and being the fastest person up and down the court was what drove me to support the starters. I knew my purpose on the team was to push the others and not rest easy. That part alone gave me a newfound excitement for myself and my teammates. My passion for running and the hard work I had done in making the opportunity to be on the team had been worth the tough journey. Those countless minutes on the treadmill and those numerous early mornings before my chores paid off handsomely in the end. There were times toward the end of the season that I was so addicted to running and feeling so fit that, if I felt we did not run enough in practice, I would head to the fitness gym and run some more on the treadmill. To say I was obsessed was an understatement.

I shudder to think what would have happened had I not chosen to be a part of the team that year. I met some amazing women and developed relationships that taught me a lot about myself. I also learned a lot from the coaches and their strong leadership – their soft-spoken demeanor and love for all of us was evident.

I learned a lot about men, too. There were some eye-opening conversations on the bus with the men's basketball players, some of whom were quite experienced in the dating world and were very open about their sexual experiences and desires. My naïve Iowa farm-girl ears were always intrigued by their stories. I felt like I had several big brothers around me at all times. I still keep in touch with one of them to this day and could not imagine not having him in my life.

Finding time in my life to stay on the team and travel, as well as do all my other activities – band, student activities, meetings, classes and fun – was a class in and of itself. In college they don't teach you Time Management 101 or Determination 202; however, I managed to achieve more in my college years than most do, simply by being a part of the team and prioritizing my life around the long and rigorous season. I thank God that my upbringing taught me to work hard and go after things I wanted with a sense of urgency that could not be matched. This made it hard for me to say no at certain points, which also compromised my life, yet it was a lesson that would strike me later during my Ironman Triathlon experience.

I continued to run even after the season ended, touring my usual 4-mile route around the small farming community. Going home that summer to my parents' farm also meant new running routes for a few months. I was up early again, going around the entire farm section this time around for the easy-to-measure square of four miles. It was wonderful to see how far much progress I had made in such a short period of time – each perfect square mile brought me effortlessly to another mile that led me to the next mile and the next. Heading back to Waldorf that fall, I was in better shape than ever before in my life.

NEW SEASONS BRING CHANGE

"People are always blaming their circumstances for what they are. I do not believe in circumstances. The people who get on in this world are the people who get up and look for the circumstances they want, and if they cannot find them, make them."

-George Bernard Shaw

After my first year of college passed, I had yet another decision to make that presented itself after my learning how to support that first season. Sitting on the bench in a supportive role had created a lot of value for me and yet, it also opened my eyes to another realization. I loved to lead. Not only did I love to lead, I also loved teamwork and synergy. I realized that we all have a vital role to play and even though I would utilize this life lesson of being support over and over again as I grew older, I also knew that my gifts were best suited in the leadership roles I would soon find myself in my sophomore year.

I opted out of basketball the second year simply because I was elected Student Body President in the spring of my freshman year after a thrilling campaign victory. I had never dappled in politics of any sort my whole life and here I was, winning the election to help govern the student body at Waldorf. Knowing that my peers trusted me with such an amazing leadership role on campus gave me the boost I wanted to make the decision I ultimately made to step down from the team.

I also wanted to devote more time to band, being 100% available there instead of being torn between basketball and band as I had been my freshman year.

I also could focus on my new love of my life. Running.

I heard a quote once by Bill Bowerman, famed University of Oregon cross country coach and founder of Nike. It started out something like, "Some would say that running is an absurd pastime in which we exhaust ourselves." Many people who knew and loved me considered it strange to spend so much time on increasing the mileage of my runs. No one in my family ran or exercised as much as I did. It appeared that I was obsessive-compulsive, back before that was a household word. Yet the thing very few people understood was how running had become my passion. Bowerman himself ended his quote, "...but if you can find meaning in the kind of running you have to do to be on this team (Oregon), perhaps you can find meaning in that other absurd pastime....life." He was so right. Running was my spiritual time with God, my meditation on the go. It led me into a world of giving and receiving support that only runners/athletes can appreciate. It gave me time alone. It gave me some of the best friends I could ever have. In fact, it was after I left my world of lone-ranger running, when I started running with my running buddy, Jared Nelson, and pursuing a life beyond just running for myself and basic conditioning, that I learned the most about myself and gained love and support from new friends.

Because of my running capacity, I became intrigued by the sport and almost wished our college had a track or cross-country team – definitely not something I would have expected from myself. Jared, a great athlete and a friend from my honors classes, began to run regularly with me that fall – he also wrestled on the college team and ran a lot anyway to stay in shape. I admired his determination and discipline. One day I saw him walking backward down a flight of stairs with a bit of a limp, or so it appeared. It turned out he had just run the Twin Cities Marathon. My first thought was, "He's crazy!" Then I realized something – I had been so quick to judge, and yet something inside of me was intrigued by the idea of running 26.2 miles, all in one shot. Subconsciously at the time I intuitively sensed that it was possible that I might want to test my limits by going through that same journey of rigorous running that he had shared with me from his own experience as a long distance runner. My mind and body and spirit were open to this possible quest.

It was Jared who signed me up for my first race. However, it was a couple of other events in my life that transformed me and stirred within me the desire to test my limits in that road race, to find that next turning point on my transformation journey.

LIFE STOPPED ON A DIME

"When a moment came and stopped me on a dime...."
-Tim McGraw song

If I thought my experience with choosing in or out of playing college basketball was a difficult situation to be in, I honestly had no idea what was to come later on. That opportunity paled in comparison to what came next for me in college – the basketball struggle merely prepared me for what was about to happen. Two back to back moments that would change the course of my future forever were on the horizon that second, pivotal year. In a song I heard once a phrase comes to mind as I write this. "A moment came and stopped me on a dime." Here is the first of two of those moments for me while at Waldorf.

It was March of 1998 and I was in Florida on a week-long band trip. My band-mate and good friend, Beth Shaw, and I were staying with a host family in Boca Raton on the night when I made a call to my parents that would change things forever.

I had been having an amazing time, and for some reason an inner voice compelled me to call my parents in Iowa to let them know what a great time I was having and see how they were. This was a very abnormal thing for me to do – I had never called my parents on any other trips in my life. I was the kid on field trips and at camp who looked at others in disgust because they were constantly calling their parents. I was too proud to admit that I even needed, or wanted, to talk to them; by not calling them, I supposedly proved my resilience and self-sufficiency.

I eagerly called and spoke with my dad and told him I was having the time of my life on our spring break in warmer temperatures. The weather in Iowa was, well, it was Iowa weather in March. As usual a bit dreary at the end of another long winter. Dad soon told me that my good friend Mike Brown had been hospitalized with an illness and that the diagnosis was acute leukemia – some type of cancer. That was all my dad knew. I said goodbye a few moments later, in utter shock at the news. I did not have any idea what either of those words meant or what the disease would hold for my friend.

"Mikey" and I had been in school together our whole lives, not unusual in our stable community. Very rarely did kids move away or move in. I did not have the fortune of getting to know Mikey very well until our high-school years, however. Boy, had I missed out. Mike was a guy who would do anything for anyone, anytime. In the fall 1995, our junior year, we formed a bond that could not be broken. We were in a drama together and spent many nights working on our lines, making pizza runs and drinking caffeine to stay awake when it wasn't our turn to be on stage. We spent time cruising the streets after play practice was over and developed a great closeness with our small circle of friends, which filled and defined our lives with love, laughter and support. Mike and I were the ringleaders. Often, we were the ones who organized the weekend get-togethers or planned the trips to see movies or go out for pizza. Because of my relationship with Mike, I also met his best friend Kyle Sipma, who would later ask me out and together we created my first real long-term relationship. Rarely was I alone with Kyle – we were like the three amigos, since Mike was a part of our relationship and Mike's girlfriend Angie was also one of my best friends.

As I got off the phone with my dad, all I could think about was Mike. Something did not feel right. My gut told me so. I felt sick to my stomach and genuinely believed that everything was not okay. I did not understand what was going on, so I frantically asked Beth and my host family what acute leukemia was. None of them knew. I asked if they had an encyclopedia or any other books that might provide some information. The Internet would have been the best tool to use, but it was hardly the reference tool it is now, so I went with what they gave me. In the dictionary they had, and "acute leukemia" was nowhere to be found, so I looked up "acute." It said plainly, "brief, sudden onset." Leukemia was not even in the dictionary; all I knew was that it was a cancer of some sort. I went to bed feeling very unsettled that night, uncertain about my friend's future: I never had come into contact with any serious illness of any kind. Mike was only 19 at the time of his diagnosis and was such a wonderful person. All I could do was stay positive and believe that he would overcome this and that God had a great plan for him.

Arriving home in Forest City the next day, I called Mikey – it was his 20th birthday, March 30th. Only a week after his initial diagnosis, he sounded very high in spirit. He was ready to get out of the hospital as soon as possible to get out on the golf course the second the snow melted. He sounded more energetic than I was, and it was hard to accept that was not in his apartment playing video games. He did not sound much different than normal, and that gave me great hope that he would, in fact, be swinging his golf clubs very soon. Within two weeks, it would be Easter break and I could see Mike in person. I did not call him the rest of that week.

On Sunday, April 5th, I arrived back at my dorm room after brunch, just in time to receive the phone call that changed the course of my life entirely. It was my high-school friend Dyan Reuvers; I was pleasantly surprised to hear from her. She had been a part of our close-knit group yet someone I rarely talked to anymore. I had no idea why she was calling, but I could tell she did not have much enthusiasm in her tone.

"Are you sitting down?" she asked as I answered the phone. I stopped short and stood still, not understanding why she would even ask that question. "No, I am not, but I can." I didn't question her seriousness, and sat down slowly, as if an old lady had taken over my body. My stomach went queasy and I felt a cold feeling enter my heart.

"Mike had died this morning" was all I heard and I remember. He had experienced complications with the leukemia. I sat there in shock – I could not move or even blink – and then it hit me. I would never see Mike again. One of the best friends I had in my whole life was no longer around. I would never get to laugh at his jokes. Never again get to rub his fuzzy, almost bald head and tease him about getting old. Never hear the desperation in his voice when he talked about not being married yet. Never see the light in his twinkling ocean-blue eyes when he told us about working with young kids at his home church. Never have those late-night conversations about our struggles in life and how much we were blessed to have our friends and family. Most importantly, I would never team up with him to plan an event with our circle of friends. Even though we had been hundreds of miles apart, we were still more committed than ever at keeping our group together on breaks and through regular communication via e-mail.

For the first time in my life, I lost all control of my emotions. Once I realized that Mikey would not be there for me on Easter break, nor any other break after that, the tears fell. My heart broke within my chest and I immediately dropped to the floor, phone still in hand. I don't remember what else Dyan said to me or whether I said anything. All I knew was that I did not want to be alone. My roommate, Brooke, was out of town, so I dashed down to the second floor of the dorm, looking for my friend Beth. I knocked on her door and barged in immediately. I ran to her and clung to her as I sobbed uncontrollably. Beth could barely understand what had happened as I attempted to explain, but I simply held on to her as hard as I could, not wanting to let go.

Before Mike, I had lost grandparents who had been considerably older than me, many of whom had died before I was even old enough to understand death. I understood that it was their time – they had lived full lives, and their time was up. Mike, on the other hand, had so much life left. I could not comprehend why he had been taken from us so soon – before he had even been married and had kids, which was his biggest dream at that moment.

My tears went on for hours. Other close friends, fortunately, were available in the dorm, including my basketball team buddy, Nate Wriedt. Nate had gotten to know Mike, as well as some of my other high-school friends, and I was relieved that he was around to listen. He was shocked and was there to help me grieve, since I needed as much support as possible. I had lost one of the most important people in my life – but I had no idea of the long-lasting impact the event would have, nor did I have any idea of the other events resulting from Mike's death that would further deepen the blow.

GOING HOME

Home is where one starts from.

-TS Elliot

Going home for Easter was a lot different than I had expected. It was the first time since my basketball decision my freshman year that I truly felt out of control of my life. I always had control of my emotions, my schedule and virtually everything around me, but I did not realize how deeply ingrained that "auto-pilot" part of me had been. I expected everything to go my way, and I could do anything when I set my mind to it. I had been protected from most things in life that could have shut down that mindset; I had been blessed with love at such a young age that I never allowed anything negative to get me down. However, the realization of life and death that I discovered on that trip home, the importance of relationships and finding closure on a life well lived all played a huge part in those next few days.

My grandparents had all died when I was really young or were not all that close to me to begin with, so when I went to their viewings at funeral homes and looked inside the coffin, it was a somber event and more scary than anything. I did not feel awful for them though because I knew they had lived long lives filled with families, great accomplishments and leaving behind a legacy filled story of their lives. Those funerals always were sad and yet I hardly ever cried or felt overwhelmed with grief as others appeared to. I understood at a young age that death was a part of life. The hard part was those that were left behind had to keep on living. I remembered when my last grandparent died when I was 14 years old. I had scheduled a weekend trip with my good friend Robyn to go with her family on a vacation to a theme park in central Iowa, called Adventureland, that very weekend my grandma passed. I knew if I stayed instead of going with my friend that I would be stuck at home with a lot of sadness and grief. Not much fun for a teenager. I also believed that she would have wanted me to go and have fun anyway. She was a peach like that. No need to stick around and mourn for someone who had lived a long life, right? That was my mindset in those experiences. Why focus on death myself, when I had so much life to yet live?

This experience was very different. My friend Nate had followed me home to attend the funeral and provide support, and I was grateful to have him by my side as I viewed Mike's body at the church. As we walked into the church to view Mike, all I could remember was the last time I saw him. That February, in the cold winter of South Dakota, I had given him a big hug as I jumped in my car to make the drive back to college. I couldn't forget that, nor will I ever forget seeing him in the coffin. I gasped as soon as I saw him lying there, lifeless and asleep for good. Missing was his usual dorky smile and twinkling eyes, always with a glimmer showing he had something up his sleeve or had just finished pulling a trick on someone. I reached out, touched the class ring on his finger and felt how stiff and cold his fingers were. I immediately started crying openly and shaking, and Nate held me and attempted to soothe me. The church was fairly vacant, and I just let out the sobs as I stood there in front of my friend. His story was still being written and his legacy had only just begun. I felt as though we were all being cheated from the best that he had yet to come.

That week itself was surreal. Attending the funeral and spending time with loved ones that I may not have seen, had Mikey not died, brought out many emotions. I still remember several of us girls piling into a car to drive out to the cemetery and never wanting to feel that anguished sorrow every again and yet the closeness that that vulnerable moment brought us to also brought us a lot closer than ever before. I left the cemetery in an exhausted daze, uncertain how our circle of friends would respond to this life changing experience. I had no idea the impact it would have on me and my relationship with my boyfriend, as well as how it would affect my next several years.

My boyfriend Kyle had not been himself at all, and I could not read his mind or even begin to know what he was feeling. Everyone cried tears and hugged and showed a variety of emotions, but I never saw Kyle shed any tears. Given the pain I was feeling, I shuddered to think how he was handling his emotions, since he was usually very good at keeping them bottled up inside.

I felt a big void in my heart, not only because of Mike, but also because of the helplessness I felt in not being able to do anything to console Kyle. I never realized that there was anything that I could do to help. I was all about fixing people and making them see that it really was not so bad. I assumed a lot about his emotions and experience. He reminded me of my father, a man who rarely showed emotions. I only had seen my father cry once in his lifetime, and that was at my grandmother's funeral. I had no idea what that could be like – I had always been able to show emotions, both happiness and sadness. I was not sure where that openness came from, but I had that gift of vulnerability at a very young age. As a kid, I cried with reckless abandon if I lost a game of Monopoly, let alone when I got into trouble. I didn't believe in bottling up emotions at that point in my life. At least not yet. That would come later after these events in college that I am describing to you now left me stunned and shaken.

Nothing I could say or do would break through to Kyle, and I returned to college with a heavy heart and a sadness that would not go away entirely. I felt confused and wanted to help him, yet could not do anything it seemed. I would have given anything to fix the situation and make him whole again.

GRADUATION

"After that came commencement day—that great day for
which all other days were made."
-Rutherford B. Hayes

I graduated with my Associate of Arts degree two short weeks later. Kyle attended and seemed to be okay in spite of what had happened. I would not return home that summer as I had the last, as I was required to continue on at Waldorf for a spring semester that began my junior year. Waldorf's Bachelor program was an accelerated 3-year program at that time in which the junior year overlapped into the third fall semester, with an internship in between the spring and fall semesters. I would graduate with my Bachelor's one summer later in 1999 after three straight semesters at the school from fall through summer. I had lined up a journalism internship in Sioux Falls, South Dakota, where Kyle lived that summer, specifically to be close to him, and I was looking forward to that prospect. I knew he was still missing his friend – we all were.

The previous summer we had taken our last vacation as a group of friends when Mike was alive. I still fondly look at those photos, reminiscing about when Mike's chair blew into our campfire, or when one of our friends locked his keys in his car and Mike would not let him live it down, or waking up in our tents in the morning and Mike bounding out with amazing energy after very little sleep.

It was on the same trip that I had first shared with Kyle my dream of marrying him. Marriage in Northwest Iowa was almost expected once one graduated from high school or college at the very least, so for me it did not seem like an odd thought at the time. Not too many people stayed single beyond age 21. For I was conditioned that if a young woman did remain single or were divorced or widowed at a young age and were on your own, you were almost considered strange or eccentric for not having a household of your very own. After dating Kyle for a year, I had already in my mind started that journey of thought as any Iowa farm girl did. The journey of marriage and living happily ever after.

I look back now and wonder if my wish for marriage was just a natural response because of my surrounding and Kyle was the lucky guy I chose to pick at the time.

It was very hard to talk openly to Kyle about that topic simply because it was a huge risk for me even to say the words, let alone think them. His response was as expected. He definitely had to think in silence for a minute after I said that full-of-commitment word – marriage – and he slowly stuttered that he had thought about it. That was all. I knew not to push and to just love him for who he was. I believe now that I was too afraid of rejection from him and my hope to pursue it any further.

I look back at that very moment today and have realized a lot. Even though I had the gumption to at least spit out the direction I wanted to go, I was afraid to scare him away and go after what I really wanted. This was new territory for me, nothing at all like the sports world or the academic world. There, I had no trouble at all taking risks, going the distance, testing the limits of my heart and mind. I had a natural ability in achieving well in sports and academia. It was matters of the heart where I was afraid of being rejected. My interpretation of failure or rejection in losing a race or getting a B did not translate over into people and relationships. I knew how easy it was to get back on the bike again after falling because I had done it so many times. However, going in the direction of relationships and expressing my true feelings was a big struggle for me. I had felt rejected at a young age by my mother who left and never let go of that memory that had been deeply planted in my body and soul. I realize now that it was not right or wrong, good or bad. It just was what it was. However, because of that deep seed that had been sown many years ago by my childhood mind, matters of the emotional heart were not my forte because of the painful consequences that I got to experience that changed my life. Unfortunately, I did not understand Kyle well enough to know that matters of the heart were difficult for him to share as well.

After my graduation I had a chance to go to France and Italy with my honors classmates. After two rigorous years devoted to our studies, presentations, tests, papers and mental anguish, we were rewarded with a trip to a country of our choice. I was glad to be able to push Mikey's death aside and travel abroad with my closest friends. The solace that gave me was priceless. I logged many running miles, exploring the back streets, nooks and crannies of some of the greatest places in the world – from Nice, France to Florence and Venice, Italy, as well as the French Riviera. My mourning process was helped by my running. I felt as though Mikey's spirit was still very much apart of me as I moved through the silence of another country in the early morning hours. Europe was fascinating, and the mystery and beauty gave me a perspective on just how big the world is. Even though I felt miles away from my distant home, I also felt very much at peace. I was able to remove myself being thousands of miles away. Again, the love and support of my friends had much to do with that. Without a doubt in my mind, I felt for the first time amazingly blessed by the people I had in my life at Waldorf that were with me, whom I knew I could call on at any given time.

When the trip was over, I managed one more trip home before heading to Sioux Falls for my summer internship at the TV station there. It was Mother's Day weekend and I was anxious to be home to see my family again and, more importantly, to visit Mikey's grave and see his family and Kyle and his family.

I had adopted Kyle's family as my own. Every Christmas, I was there for part of the celebration and really fell in love with his aunts, uncles and cousins, not just his immediate family. I had visions of spending the rest of our remaining years celebrating family events, and I was thankful that my family approved of him as well.

That Sunday, I left my family and spent some of the afternoon with Kyle's before the 2 ½-hour drive back to college. Kyle managed to be somewhat his old self again although I could tell that, in just those short 30 days since Mike's funeral, Kyle had lost a startling amount of weight from his already thin frame.

As I was getting ready to leave, he said something about coming to meet me at Waldorf that night to talk in person about something important. I had no idea what it could be. What could be so important that he could not bring it up right then and there? I did not ask him – actually, I was thankful that he was finally reaching out to me after a month of uncertainty and silence.

I arrived at my dorm room after dark. I had no roommate at the time, and the campus was a ghost town since only juniors, seniors and part-time students were still attending class. My room was fairly bare since my roommate, Brooke, had left and we had removed much of the furniture. I had grown to love my dorm room – 315 North Tanner Hall. It overlooked the entire campus and we had a beautiful oak tree that gave us some shade and touched our window. That room held many memories from my two years there, and it was to be the last month I would live there. One more memory would be created that night when Kyle arrived.

It was roughly 9 p.m. when he entered my dorm room. I was somewhat anxious and apprehensive, still in amazement that he was making a six-hour round trip just to talk to me. Whatever he wanted to talk about was well worth the extra hours on the road. As he took a seat across from me as I sat on the bed, I felt a sinking filling in my stomach. I had never seen such an expression on his face. He looked very somber, brooding, struggling to look me straight in the eyes. We held hands in the silence, which he broke with words that shocked me to my core: He did not want to date anymore and felt our relationship was over.

As soon as I started crying, he almost did as well and had to look away for a moment. I asked him why and what we could do to keep things going between us – I did not want to let go. He had no real explanation, and that made it even harder. I did not want to bring up Mike, yet all I could think of was that his death had a lot to do with Kyle's decision. My heart was breaking once again. I believed at the time that he was not thinking clearly and that his grief was causing him to make wrong choices. Yet at that same moment I knew why he had driven all that way to break the news to me – his love and concern for me. For my own safety, he did not want me driving after our break-up.

Boy, was that the right decision – I was devastated beyond belief. First I had lost Mike, and now I was losing Kyle, the man whom I had thoughts of marriage. He told me what an amazing woman I was and that he was the right one for me. Once my mind and body went numb and we had spent some moments hugging, he left. Before he had even left the building, I fell to my knees in an emotional outburst.

Mike's death was still fresh in my mind, and when I cried tears of frustration after Kyle left, I did not just cry for Kyle – I also had fresh tears of grief from Mike. It was like receiving another deep cut on a fresh wound that had not even begun to heal. I had no idea what the three-hour drive back to Sioux Falls was like for Kyle – I was just grateful I did not have to go anywhere.

As when the news of Mike had reached me, I knew this was not a good time to be alone. There weren't many students on campus, yet the ones there were my best friends, and I sought them out. As I ran out of my dorm and into the darkness, I could barely see through the tears streaming down my face. I nearly knocked over a young woman who was walking up the stairs as I was sprinting down, but I could not even mutter an apology: my sobs were all I could muster.

I arrived at the room of my friends, Kaylee and Mandy, sobbing as they opened the door. I collapsed onto their futon and continued to wail. They could barely understand what I said, yet they got the basic idea that Kyle had broken up with me. It took me several minutes even to calm down and share what had caused me to be in so much pain and sadness. They both knew about Mike and were visibly concerned, and it felt great to have them there, drying my tears, holding me on their futon. At one point, Kaylee even wondered aloud whether I should have some type sedative. I actually cracked a smile at that, and they offered me some hot chocolate instead. Kaylee told me later that I had even wanted to drive all the way to Sioux Falls to see if Kyle had changed his mind. I thought I could do something to get us back together. I had no idea how that moment would impact me for the next 7 years of my life.

MOVING FORWARD IN THE RACE OF LIFE

"Our thoughts, beliefs and emotions create our reality."
- Unknown

That summer, spent in the same city as Kyle, was a rough one. As was usual for me, I stayed busy to numb the pain, working two jobs and my internship, though I had no idea that was what I was doing. My running was more important to me than ever, and I became even more focused on it. It was the key to my void.

As a result of all that I went through, even up to today, I can now look at painful, life-changing events as though I am a vine branch in a vineyard. Whenever the pruning process takes place, it is in order to cut back the overgrowth of that vine to allow new growth and productivity in other areas. I did not realize then what the loss of the two closest men in my life would mean for my beliefs about being worthy of a close relationship with a man, yet it was an area to which I would close myself for 7 years. The walls around my heart were erected and emotional running took on a whole new look.

Kyle, on the other hand, had appeared to move on and had started another relationship not too long after we broke up. I chose to stay single and endure through my heartache – not letting go. Yet, this was a choice that I made for myself. I see that now when I look back and reflect on that period of my life. In all other areas of my life, I had moved on. Dating, however, was nonexistent. The pain was still far too deep. I had not had a relationship in over a year and, deep down chose not to for a long time. The walls around my heart had not so much as cracked. Subconsciously, I learned recently, that moment reminded me a lot of when my mom left and moved on when I was a child. I felt abandoned. I felt cheated. And even though it was painful beyond measure, I chose to hold on to that pain after the death and my break up because it was familiar. It was what I knew all too well and it served me to a degree because if I did not allow myself to love again, then I also would not allow myself to feel pain again. I was covering myself up as if in a cocoon, not wanting to come out as a butterfly. Not wanting to transform. Not wanting to change. Wanting to find other things to feel that all too painful void. That old adage about, "'Tis better to have loved and lost than to not have loved at all" did not appeal to me at that time. I was fine being the lone ranger, independent and pain free, focusing all my time and energies on other things. Soon, another event would happen that helped take my mind off of the pain.

MY FIRST RUN

"We all have big changes in our lives that are more or less a second chance."
-Harrison Ford

The two areas that were being pruned on my own vine after Mike's death and Kyle's breaking up with me, were my physical and spiritual branches, which took me in a whole a new direction in life. It was May of 1998, one month after Mike died and two weeks after Kyle broke the news, when I ran my first road race, a 5 mile-run in Mason City, Iowa. I had never before felt in my running as accomplished as I did on that day. I am sure that the events of the previous month had something to do with that.

In the race, I had expended all the energy I had, running in all cotton on a hot and humid Midwest day, sporting my two-year old basketball sneakers. Needless to say, I had novice written all over me. I had no idea there was such a thing as proper running attire for a running competition, or that you shouldn't use non-running shoes that had probably a thousand miles on them. I still have pictures of the finish, my face red with exhaustion and sweat.

Looking closer at that face, you can also see excitement and a look of determination. I had found something that gave a whole new meaning to my life, something that would lead me on a journey to my first triathlon and, eventually, to the Ironman Triathlon. Something clicked in me. I had thrived on the rush of being in the pack with men and women all pursuing a common goal.

As I raced I thought of Mike, as I always had on my runs since April 5th, truly believing that he was with me every step of the way. Ironically enough, that first race was named after and held in memory of a man named Stu Nevermann, who had died of cancer at around the same age as Mike. That bittersweet moment set me up for something even greater later on.

That fall, I also signed up for my first half-marathon race. 13.1 miles was something I had never run before but yet seemed so attainable. The race, funnily enough, was in Sioux Falls, and some friends and family were there to cheer me on. The finish was less than a mile from where Mike and Kyle had lived together, and the memories were fresh the whole way I ran. The finish was exhilarating and again an affirmation of my passions of running and finishing a goal I started.

Never before had I felt so fulfilled. As Eric Liddell says in the famed running movie, *Chariots of Fire*, "I believe God made me for a purpose, but he also made me fast. And when I run I feel His pleasure." When I first heard that quote, I got goosebumps. It completely resonated with me – I could sense my life continuing to head in an amazing direction. My running was a part of who I was not only physically but also spiritually.

After finishing that half-marathon and winning first-place female at my college's homecoming 5K that fall, I continued to run. Even through the deadly winter months, I was devoted. Others thought I was crazy to don multiple layers – scarves, thick gloves and stocking cap – as I trekked through wind, snow, ice, even in the middle of blizzards. I would do whatever it took to complete my training. I planned on returning to the Stu Nevermann race again to see if all the running I had done through the elements had made me a heartier runner. I believed that my dedication and determination would pay off. I was right once again.

As I toed the line for my second running of the 5-mile Mason City race, I knew in my heart that I was in better shape. My confidence was high and my race that day showed it.

By the finish, it was clear that I had improved in two areas. One, I had improved my time by a whopping 5 minutes, roughly one minute per mile, and two, I was the first female to cross the line. I finished ahead of every other woman who had showed up that day, and I brought home a trophy to show for it. I was ecstatic, to say the least. I began to see possibilities and dreams of being even faster, better, stronger; I saw the Olympics looming in my future. I was excited and energized, seeing past any limits in myself.

Once again, I was touched by the story of Stu Nevermann and remembered silently my friend Mikey as I crossed the finish line. Once again, I was grateful that I could focus on my memory of Mike, thanking him for creating in me a desire to keep moving forward in my life. I still cried for my friend on a regular basis when I ran, or even when I didn't. I could simply hear a story or a song that reminded me of him and the tears would flow. I still missed him terribly.

A NIGHT TO REMEMBER

"Today if the first day of the rest of my life."
-Unknown

In July of 1999, just shy of my Bachelor's Degree graduation, I experienced another major turning point of my life, one that I had not predicted but that would be the next step in my Ironman journey.

I heard about a meeting of the Leukemia Society of America (LSA), a non-profit organization raising funds and awareness to find a cure for leukemia, a blood-related cancer. I was drawn to the meeting because I wanted to find out how I could honor Mike by making a difference to those still battling the disease that took his life at the tender age of 20.

That night I learned about how I could run a marathon (26.2 miles) and raise nearly $4,000 to go toward the research of a cure for leukemia. I was transfixed by a video describing the program and giving testimonials from people who had achieved their marathon/fundraising goals. The tears fell from my eyes at the smiles of the patients were battling the illness who were "adopted" by the Team in Training group as their honorees. The stories were shared among the attendees of the meeting, and I found solace in knowing that I was not alone in losing someone I loved to leukemia. My heart raced as I left the meeting that night, and I was silent on the ride home. I had signed up to run 26.2 miles in Walt Disney World on January 9, 2000. I felt that what happened that night changed my future in a big way – little did I know where it would take me next.

Training for and running my first marathon taught me a lot about myself, inside and out. It taught me about overcoming obstacles, training all by myself (this was before I joined a running club and racing team), running through bad winter weather, and getting up on many dark and cold mornings and dressing for the elements. I was training for an event, devoted to a cause much higher than myself. Not only did I have running obstacles, but I had moved out of my home state to a new and somewhat foreign city, Minneapolis. Not knowing more than a handful of people made it difficult to raise the funds for the cause. I didn't let that stop me, however. I not only reached the financial goal given to me by LSA, I exceeded it through the giving of many generous people.

MY FIRST MARATHON

"This is the beginning of a new day. God has given me this day to use as I will. I can waste it – or use it for good, but what I do today is important, because I am exchanging a day of my life for it!"

-Dr. Heartstill Wilson

That first marathon is still imprinted in my brain. I flew from Minneapolis to Orlando, Florida, with much excitement and confidence; I had been preparing for this moment for the past three years and was amazed at how perfect the timing had been. I began to realize that there was no such thing as coincidence and that God's timing in my life had transcended all else.

Throughout my own love and dedication to the cause, I saw and felt my own inner transformation. My body experienced change through the physical dedication, and I truly had no other motive to take part in this event other than Mikey. Even the unity it brought between his family and myself was an amazing gain. The Brown family had chosen to be in Orlando to watch me complete the marathon. Knowing they were there and being able to greet them at the finish line was huge. I felt their love and was grateful to see their joy-filled smiles – Mikey was living on in spirit, and we were paying tribute to him.

In those 26.2 miles through Walt Disney World, I was running with other LSA fundraising runners who had the same goal. Knowing that we had altogether raised over a $1 million was also gratifying – it displayed what the Team in Training name really represented. We achieved more together than alone. I ran with one particular LSA gentleman who had the same time goal of 3 hours and 30 minutes. Kevin was from New York and I had never met him before; however, LSA brought us together and we ran a majority of the race together. We paced each other until roughly mile 18 when he really started cramping up and could not keep the same pace. It was then that I moved forward on my own.

Yet I knew I was not alone. Mikey was with me those last several miles, as he always was on my runs, and one of the most amazing events happened at mile 21. It was roughly at that point when I truly started feeling "The Wall", the infamous point in the marathon where you struggle with continuing to move forward. It's almost as if a brick wall is standing right in front of you, holding you back from finishing – a psychological point of no return. Your mind at this point is playing tricks on you, telling you to give up. Not believing in yourself is the worst possible thing because it can cause you to self destruct.

At my wall I was really missing my pacing friend, Kevin, who had been there for me so many miles. My legs were feeling like lead as I entered into new territory: the most mileage I had run to prepare for this day was 21 miles, and now I was going beyond that point. Yet my guardian angel showed up just in the nick of time. My mind started the destructive and negative self talk to my body, where my inner self was battling with the outer, attempting to control it, forcing me to stop. "You can't do this" and "What's the point" were a few things firing in my head. I found myself running at the side of a man whom I could tell was struggling just as much as I was, if not more. I totally empathized with him, and we struck up a conversation. Turned out he was using that marathon as a training run for another one in New Orleans a few weeks later. He planned to run only 23 miles and then drop out. This was the first time I had ever heard such a crazy idea, and I truly was horrified at the thought of just using a marathon as a training run. There would be no crossing the finish line. No Mickey Mouse medal! At the same time, I admired him for his dedication to the sport and creating an experience in and of itself. I also was grateful for him being there for what happened next.

After a moment of silence, I asked his name, and my heart skipped a beat when he told me: Mike. Mike was his name. I smiled to myself. I was looking for some encouragement from somewhere at this point in my run, and it had appeared in the shape of a man named Mike. Just before we parted ways, he slowed, checked his watch and told me something that would change my life in a big way: I was on pace. I asked, "Pace for what?" Qualifying for

Boston, he said. Being a true newbie, I had no clue at what he meant. He explained that the Boston Marathon was the most prestigious marathon in the world – everyone who ran in it had to qualify by running a certain time in another marathon that was sanctioned or chosen as a qualifying marathon. I was on pace to eclipse my goal time of 3:30 by several minutes and if I kept that up, he said, I would easily beat the 3:40 qualifying time for women my age. I was pretty tired, and I did not really know the scale of what he was talking about – otherwise, I would have been celebrating. As I found out later, many runners would kill to have been in my shoes at that moment and there I was, not even having a clue!

Not only did I finished the event, collapsing into the arms of Mike's family, I eclipsed the Boston qualifying time I needed by 20 minutes. Doing so well and experiencing the finish with the Browns gave me even more purpose and meaning. I was flying high and no one was going to take me down.

I went on to run the 2000 Boston Marathon and even fundraised for yet another LSA marathon in Anchorage, Alaska, that June. I was on a mission and did not want to slow down. A 5-year-old boy named Luke at my newspaper workplace, battling leukemia, inspired to be putting another name to my list of honored patients who were still alive fighting the good fight. I placed first in my age group at the Alaska event and was able to meet Christine

Clark, the 2000 Olympic marathoner from Anchorage. Again, I was inspired and received benefits I would have never partaken in if I had not continued moving forward in my pursuit of a great cause.

I rounded out my marathon year with my fourth marathon in my own backyard – the Twin Cities – on a course that I could have run in my sleep. An interdenominational faith prayer service the morning of the race inspired me for the journey ahead. I planned to run with my college buddy Jared. We would pace each other the whole way and qualify him for Boston, which meant a time of 3 hours 10 minutes. That would be a huge jump for him and a good-sized jump for me. Yet he had been there for me so many times, supporting me in getting to that first start line, that I was determined to see him achieve his goal.

We paced each other easily until mile 13, and at the halfway point, Jared began to struggle. I could see he was truly fighting a physical and mental battle to keep the pace. He told me to go ahead and run on my own, but I struggled at first because a huge part of me did not want to leave my friend. Then there was a voice inside of me, seemingly selfish, that wanted to keep going and test my limits – I wanted to see what my body could do.

The night before, I had watched a movie about the life of running legend Steve Prefontaine. The story of his life and death moved me beyond measure and stays with me even to this day. He ran with a passion and a drive that could not be matched by anyone else. He believed that if he did not give an all-out, 100% effort in every single race, he was cheating himself as a runner and all who witnessed the run. Not many runners or even people in general, have that philosophy, and just to see his story on the screen gave me a new appreciation of living life to the fullest and giving everything and everyone your all. His famous quote, "To give anything less than your best is to sacrifice the Gift", sums up his legacy. He never gave less than his best.

I gave my all that beautiful fall day in October: I left Jared behind and stayed on pace for the 3:10 finish. At mile 18, as I crossed the Lake Street Bridge over the Mississippi River, I felt a slight twinge in my right foot. I had never felt that pain before; however, I had started feeling some foot pain in my training, and I wondered if this pain was related. I pushed through the pain and past any wall that came my way. As I raced up Summit Ave, the infamously long hill between miles 21 and 25, for what seemed like forever, I saw some familiar faces in the crowd cheering me on and I kept pace, plugging forward despite the pain.

I finished in almost exactly 3:10. I was overwhelmed with elation and remember clearly saying, "That was easy!" My friend and running companion, Bob Malmgren, and his wife, Denise, picked me up and brought me home. He just laughed and shook his head when he heard me say that, but I truly felt strongly that I could have done better, and I still had aspirations to shoot for the moon by qualifying for the Olympic marathon.

In the week that followed, however, my dream was altered a bit. The twinge at mile 18 had been more than just that. The foot pain I had noticed the few weeks leading up to the marathon did not go away. I would wake up with the pain in the morning, and walking was difficult as soon as my feet hit the ground from my bed. I could run, yet not pain-free until after the first mile warm-up. I started to suspect this was not just a minor pain that would go away on its own.

Yes, the sport of triathlon chose me – I did not choose it. I had been biking quite a bit during my years in Minneapolis, even biking to work every day. Every day, through rain, snow, wind or ice, I would bundle myself up and cruise the ten-mile round trip. I purchased my first road bike from Jeff Shea, a fellow marathoner. He said that this Cannondale road bike was the same one he had used for his Hawaii Ironman experience, which he explained was the granddaddy of all triathlons: a 2.4-mile swim, a 112-mile bikeride, topped off with a 26.2-mile marathon distance run – all in one day! I was in awe how of someone who could do an event so intense and so long! It took all day, and I had thought marathoners were crazy!

Yet a surprising curiosity entered my mind as I stood in Jeff's living room, reliving the experience through his photos. I thought, "Hey, I could probably do that if I put my mind to it." I didn't know when, where or how, but deep inside I felt the same feeling as when I heard about marathon races. I had found a new challenge and a new goal, something above and beyond myself – and something not many people would venture to do.

IRONMAN INTRIGUE

"As long as you're going to think anyway, think big."
-Donald Trump

After purchasing Jeff's bike, I had a vision of becoming a triathlete. But I had some trepidations about avoiding running while I figured out what was wrong with my feet. I could see that cross training and looking for alternatives had its benefits. I still believed nothing could come close to running with the adrenaline rush and ultimate high I felt, however, reason told me that I had overdone it the past couple years and my body was telling me something.

Time off from a sport that has become a part of you is a hard thing. The runner's addiction is almost a parallel addiction to a drug junkie's. Once you experience the runner's high, there is no turning back. The fear of becoming complacent and out of shape dominates the obsessive-compulsive athlete. I was blessed with a very high pain threshold and even though both of my feet experienced pain from the moment I awoke, I still managed to hobble through some mileage. But by December, the pain had become so debilitating that I had to stop.

I timidly asked Jeff how I could start swimming, since I saw him as my triathlon guru. He immediately invited me to attend his

Master's swim sessions at a local college. At first, I was really excited – but that excitement waned to intimidation when I showed up for my first early morning session. I hadn't though about what the word "Master's" meant. However, Jeff assured me I would be fine. In my one-piece suit with a few years of use on it, I felt like the ugly duckling in a bunch of swans – I did not even have a swim cap or goggles at the time! Jeff had to supply those for me. As I stood there, feeling out of place, each person did warm-up stretches that were foreign to this runner. I had swimming experience, but my pre-lifeguard training did nothing to prepare me for this. These swimmers looked like Olympic professionals, swinging their arms first clockwise and then counter-clockwise around their bodies. I can't even describe the other warm-ups they did: it was that impressive. As they did their warm-up laps, I could only muster about one and a half. I had hardly ever been in the beginner group in any sport. Intimidated by the cost of the course ($40/month) and the others' abilities, I gave it up by the end of October, sticking with my daily bike rides to my job at the newspaper in downtown Minneapolis.

Jeff reassured me that I could come a few times to get a feel of the class before signing up, if at all. I did attend a few more times and each time was more and more intimidated at the level of experience each person had. I felt eons behind them in their abilities and did not know if I could stay committed to the daily 6 a.m. swim classes.

In addition, I finally gave up running altogether that winter because the pain was too great, and I started pursuing help from every angle. First, I went to a physical therapist for a few weeks of therapy. I was diagnosed with plantar fasciitis, which turned out to be the most common cause of heel pain. The plantar fascia is the flat band of tissue that connects your heel bone to your toes and supports the arch of your foot. If you strain your plantar fascia, it gets weak, swollen, and irritated, or inflamed, and your heel or the bottom of your foot hurts when you stand or walk. Plantar fasciitis is common in middle-aged people, and it also occurs in younger people who are on their feet a lot, like athletes or soldiers.

The physical therapist referred me to a foot doctor, who made me orthotics for my running shoes. I took yoga for a month in December, which gave me more relief than anything else; that told me it had to be a balance or stretching issue. I was not 100%, but I did return to some light running in January. Yet once I stopped doing yoga regularly, I was back to square one. I did manage to get in some swimming again, as well as some water aerobics classes, to keep moving toward my triathlon goal .

Another physical therapist tried cortisone shots and prescribed a boot that I could wear at night to alleviate the pain. The boot actually did work – however, I only had one boot and two feet, and the pain came back in full force when the boot was off. I was beginning to think my running career was over. It did not help to hear at the same time that a few professional athletes in the NBA and NFL had chosen not to retire because of plantar fasciitis diagnoses. But despite all that, I was determined not to give up.

I truly missed running, to the depths of my soul. It was such an important part of my day, but it just wasn't the same with pain involved. I wanted to do another Leukemia Society event to raise more funds for Mike's memory and for Luke, the little boy who was still battling the disease. I found out that the Minnesota LSA chapter was training during the winter/spring of 2001 for a "century" (100-mile) training ride in Lake Tahoe, California. With my current biking abilities and my Ironman road bike, I felt compelled to sign up and raise funds yet again – only this time on wheels.

I was excited about the opportunity to move forward in this newfound discipline, and I attacked my new sport with excitement and fully embraced the challenge. As when I started running, I mostly did my training on my own. I went anywhere and everywhere on my bike – we were inseparable. My co-workers thought I was insane to pedal through snow, freezing temperatures and the dark of night, no matter what. I did not care what others thought – I was a lone ranger, and once again, I had a mission, a purpose to accomplish.

LONLINESS OF THE LONG DISTANCE RUNNER

"A mask to disguise him. A great silver stallion and thus began his fame. Hi-yo silver, away!"
-From Lone Ranger and Tonto

Lone Ranger. That word truly fits most runners out there. There's even a book about it. "Loneliness of the Long Distance Runner". Solitude in running can be done in almost a meditative state. I had grown so accustomed to running by myself that it was more normal for me to be running solo than with a group. Biking, I found, was a very similar concept. I was single-minded in my purpose for both sports and grew a lot in that time. When my mind has plenty of time to wander and process the meaning of life in deep thought as the adrenaline and blood pumps throughout the body, something magical happens and I would notice regularly that I would have my best thoughts while running. My spiritual connectivity would flow and I would many times wish that I had a tape recorder along with me on my run as I created amazing ideas that were undoubtedly significant for one area of my life. I would dream up new ideas for my business or prepare in my mind ways to solve problems or plan on how to approach a conversation with a loved one. Surrounded by the beauty of nature and connecting with my inner drive and passion, I have witnessed some life changing events.

When I became a running coach for the Life Time Fitness Running Club in Minneapolis, MN in the latter part of 2000, it was something new for me to be the leader of a group of people that wanted to achieve certain running/fitness goals. It was a leadership opportunity, at the tender age of 22, that would chart a new course in an exciting direction for me. It was on these group runs that I also noticed how not only my transformation took place, rather the transformation of others. The ironic thing about running is this. If you are out on a run with someone there is no place to hide physically, or better yet, emotionally or spiritually. Because of that I have had many deep, thought provoking conversations with people. I would see the true side of someone on the running trails or even bike rides that others may not see in the office or sadly enough, even at home. Once the juices were flowing, people became more open. More vulnerable. More willing to share.

This is why I think that is. We were born to run as children. The playful nature of running brings out in most people the best of their true selves. Many forms of exercise are seen as stress relievers or reducers, so when one moves with the flow of our bodies in the manner of our forefathers that traveled the earth on foot, we are at one with ourselves. That is what I believe for myself and find that everyone I know that commits to running, those that really want to do it to accomplish a goal or for a cause or purpose, it is those that find great reward. This can be compared to any commitments we make in life, not just athletic endeavors. This was a key lesson for me to learn at a young age.

On those many runs with my new running club members we talked about life. Everything from divorce to death to job layoffs. We celebrated marriages, new home purchases, holiday parties, going away parties, new babies. We had a community of our own and connected to such a deep level that to this day I still keep in touch with every single person that I was close with from my original running club, as well as other clubs that I joined or built since that initial group. We broke bread together, we drank together, we road tripped together, we dreamed together, we encouraged each other at races, we cried when injuries sidelined us, we laughed when we ran in our Halloween costumes for our group run or made snow angels in the winters. I was more alive in my life at that time than many others because of the relationships, love and true purpose all of that goodness gave me. I remember even one moment in the middle of a run in the cold morning hours when not many people were around, one gentleman told me about his frustrations with his fear for his wife's health and for the future of their five children without a mom who could take care of them. His voice was filled with so much anguish that even I started crying. We stopped at a very scenic place and just talked and then even said a prayer together. I'll never forget that moment as long as I live. I'll always remember that man and even today wonder how things are going for him.

FIRST TRIATHLON

"Beyond familiar...just past fear...that's where life expands."

- Unknown

I joined small group bike rides with my LSA teammates once the spring thaw brought out the rest of the riders. By May I was in tip top shape, raised more than enough money to eclipse the goal and trekked to the Tahoe century with excitement at the new venture my team would embark upon in traveling 100 miles around perhaps the most beautiful lake in the world. My step-brother, John, came and joined me for the event and I spent as much time visiting with him as well. He has always been a big part of my support system as well through many of my athletic endeavors. I saw a similar camaraderie amongst the riding group as I had in my running club, which expanded upon my original experience I had with team sports in high school. Together everyone really did achieve more.

It was August of 2001 that I took part in my first triathlon event. The Brewhouse Triathlon in Duluth, Minnesota. August can be a very hot and humid time for the Midwest, even up in northern Minnesota. This was the land of the mosquitoes, which we jokingly dubbed the state bird. Many a tale was told of people being carried off by these monstrous creatures that wanted nothing more than to suck a human's blood in the summer heat. That hot and sultry day did not allow me to be overly competitive, which was perfect. I was able to sit back and cruise through my first tri event with ease, which was not my normal nature. I had joined racing team in Minneapolis in 2000 and I definitely was used to racing at full throttle, not holding anything back. For my first triathlon though I was able to put things in a different perspective. I had no clue how long the transitions between the three events were to take, had no expectation on where I would finish in what time, let alone what place in my age group and I had traveled up to the race with some fellow Life Time Fitness friends who were just wanting to finish the race. By the time I reached the run, I could not even run the whole event for fear of dying of heat stroke or exhaustion. I had to pour two ice cold glasses of water over my head at every mile marker to stop me from passing out. Some might call me crazy for loving my experience simply from hearing that news about the heat obstacle. However, I felt even more accomplished and excited that I had achieved that awesome goal in the midst of adverse conditions.

This entry into the triathlon world truly gave me a new perspective on the world of racing events. I witnessed so many people of different shapes and sizes in this triathlon than I ever had in any running or biking event. The variety of ages and abilities was refreshing. It truly was a testament at how this sport was open for all people. Anyone could achieve it if they simply believed in themselves and went out and did it. Just as in life. I immediately found a home in this new arena and definitely wanted to sign up for another race. I just didn't know where or when. It did not end up being until a full year later for the first annual Life Time Fitness Triathlon in Minneapolis in 2002.

Another benefit of the triathlon that I noted over just running or biking alone, was the overall condition of my body. My plantar fasciitis was much less affected, even though still there. My body physically appeared to gain more benefit as well as I looked more well rounded. When just running, I knew that I looked a bit under nourished and rail thin. Just biking focused more on my lower body strength in my legs and butt. Throwing in swimming was beneficial as it worked yet even other areas that did not receive any attention from the other two disciplines. Water itself is over 700 times more resistant than air, so the overall body conditioning was a HUGE benefit. I noticeably gained more muscle mass and strength, which was needed to go the distance.

Swimming was by far still my weakest link. It was actually something that I feared. I did not tell anyone that and did not even admit it to myself until recently. At that first triathlon lake swim, I was third to last out of the water. This was a new place for me to be. I knew I had some rather large limiting beliefs about myself in that discipline. I even, on occasion, had anxiety attacks in the water because of my unfamiliarity, lack of skill and fear. I knew that this sport was foundational in technique, so you had to have some coaching and continue to practice it regularly in order to master it. I still had not made the commitment to signing up for any coaching or swimming groups. After the experience with Jeff's Masters swim team, that was still territory I could not embrace. I was stubborn. I did not understand why I could not master this on my own, since I had done that so easily in the other two disciplines of running and biking. My lone ranger capabilities had gained a lot of ground for me there. I knew in order for me to improve in the swim, I would have to reach out and find help. I spoke to many coaches in the area and found that their prices could not fit into my budget at the time, so I did the next best thing. I asked friends that I knew were good swimmers to give me some pointers. Going off of their advice, I would practice on my own, at best two times a week. This was not much of a training regimen for me to follow given I continued to take part in a much larger balance of running and biking, however, I made it work. It's funny how we athletes tend to gravitate toward the easier sports that we naturally excel at. It is very much human nature to not focus on weaknesses and celebrate strengths. Someone might argue that in the sport of triathlon as long as you had two out of three mastered, you were on your way to success. However, true to my competitive nature, I knew that I did not want to be seen as mediocre in any one area. I knew in my heart that I would master swimming or die trying.

Upon receiving some tidbits of knowledge from my friends in the swimming world, I was able to make it through that second triathlon with much more confidence on the swim than I had before. I still had not needed a wetsuit as it was in a warm Minnesota lake and that made it less intimidating. The bike and run went phenomenally well and my gifts of perseverance and discipline for this three disciplined sport continued to send me into the direction of my first Ironman Triathlon.

ARIZONA

"A hundred ten in the shade is sorta hot, but you don't have to shovel it off your driveway."
~Author Unknown

Before I explain my transition to Phoenix from Minneapolis, I want to share why I chose this Southwestern state to move to in embarking upon a new adventure in my mid-twenties.

At a young age I became enamored with Phoenix, Arizona. This love and curiosity for this city came from my days of watching Charles Barkley play basketball when he made his switch from the Philadelphia 76ers to the Suns of Phoenix. I had no other reason to adopt that team than that.

As my brother, Rich, and I would sit in our toasty warm recliners with our jeans, socks and long sleeves, I was tantalized by the scenery of Phoenix on the television screen. This had nothing to do with what was going on inside the America West Arena, the basketball gymnasium where the Suns took to hard court. It had everything to do with the camera shots of people walking around in shorts outside amongst palm trees and beautiful desert landscape. Whenever we caught a glimpse of the city lights at the setting of the Phoenix sun, I was entranced by the idea of some day visiting this beautiful state. I was sure that it was paradise, a sort of Heaven on earth that not everyone got to visit or see in person. It seemed too far away for me, a farm girl sitting in Iowa, and yet I felt this tug in my heart that I would some day be there, in that very arena in fact. A dream had been born. A land without snow, ice and offered up year round tanning opportunities. I was in love.

As the other divine moments of my dreams born as a child, where God created the person or persons to fulfill that dream, it was several years later that my opportunity to visit Phoenix and the America West Arena became a reality.

It was while I was in Paris, France with my college friends during my sophomore honors trip that I met Bill and Judy Murphy in the lobby of the Hotel Kensington. I had raced down the steep, narrow wooden stairs of our hotel to check in with the hotel desk clerk about the goings on of the NBA playoffs in the United States. I had no idea why I believed that a Frenchman would know anything about American professional basketball and yet my driven curiosity was killing me. As I threw my hands up in the air at the lack of answers from the desk man, I whirled around and my eyes landed upon a group of older travelers that were obviously from the U.S. My heart leapt with joy when I saw that one of the gentlemen donned a Suns baseball cap. I quickly ran over to his side and asked him if he knew anything about the outcome of the recent playoff game. His smile said it all. They knew exactly what was going on and I found out they were season ticket holders with rights to second row seats at every home game. Two rows from the floor where the professionals took the court. I was dumbfounded by the opportunity.

I happily took Judy's business card and with one look at their smiling and trusting faces, I completely fell in love and knew that we had made a connection that went deeper than just that one moment. I knew I would see them again some day.

That some day came less than a year later.

Waldorf College had required me to have two internships during my time there and the last to be done in the spring of 1999. I dreamed of calling up a Phoenix TV station and asking to be a part of the sports department. That dream became a reality once I remembered Bill and Judy's offer of taking me to a Suns game if I ever visited Phoenix. I called them up and took the opportunity to ask if I could stay with them during my potential six week internship. They were my first call to secure housing. On my limited college budget, I was doing everything I could to create the perfect situation for myself. The Murphys came through and offered up free lodging, as well as at least one visit to see the Suns!!

While there for those 6 weeks, I felt at home. I believe in my heart that this was the perfect place and time for me to be there, experiencing a new city. I waitressed at a local mom and pop Italian restaurant called "Mamma Mia's", which funny enough was owned and operated by an Iranian family. Being from Iowa, that struck me as odd and yet I was intrigued by the life of the big city.

I fulfilled my dream of going to a Suns game, getting to cover some games and be available to cover sports in the sweaty locker rooms of the arena, be escorted by my very own security guard at night in downtown Phoenix at the Fox station I interned at and rub shoulders with one of the top television market's nightly newscasts. I was in my element. The weather was not bad either. Being in Phoenix in late February and all of March was the best time to be there. I went back to Iowa as dark as an olive skinned European! Many of my family and friends were jealous. Leaving Phoenix was bittersweet and yet I knew I would be back there some day. That much was clear in my mind and heart. I just did not know the 'how'.

Fast forward. In the winter of 2002, my move to Phoenix came. Unknowingly the city was a thriving triathlete community. The sport was just taking off there with many professional triathletes living or residing in this year-round training community. Within my first month of moving there I met a triathlon coaching company, called 1st Triathlon. I ended up coaching for them and being introduced to some top notch swim coaches. Being outside for an evening swim workout in January boggled my mind when just two short months prior I was in freezing temperatures in the Midwest. I was loving it!

Not really being back into full force running yet due to my continued plague of plantar fasciitis, I looked at my triathlon future in a different light. I noted that there were plenty of races locally, as well as learned that many triathletes traveled to cities in California such as San Diego, Malibu and Los Angeles and Las Vegas, Nevada to experience other opportunities in the racing arena. I even met up with a couple aspiring triathletes, J'aime Sans Souci and Tina King, that became great friends at my real estate office and we traveled to California and did a couple triathlons there my first two years in Arizona.

Moving to Arizona also developed in me all sorts of new training techniques. One extreme change had to do with my sleeping habits. I had always been an early-morning person from my days, but with the Phoenix heat, the West-Coast lifestyle, and coaching other marathon runners, my idea of early morning wake-up calls was totally transformed. No longer did 5:30 or 6 a.m. look early to me; I grew accustomed to 5 o'clock, or even as early as 4:00 on some occasions. I remember waking at 3:30 one morning to log in a 20-mile run because I had to be at the airport by 9 a.m. that day.

I definitely had to adjust my habits with friends – staying out late was now 10 p.m., not midnight.

Fast forward to June 2004, when I heard that the Ironman Triathlon was coming to Tempe. In fact, the start/finish line was roughly 2.5 mile from my house. I couldn't believe it! Thanks to my personal trainer, Jase Graber, I had overcome a lot (plantar fascitis, runner's knee, and heel spurs just to name a few) and was virtually injury-free after four years of physical therapy and trying everything short of surgery. Another advantage was the close proximity of Ironman Arizona, so I didn't have to worry about traveling to the event and carting along my bike/wetsuit/etc. Plenty of my fellow LifeTime Fitness members were signing up for the event, as were those in my triathlon cycling club. I was not alone.

This was a big goal for anyone – I knew that this was a serious event, one I would have to respect and not take lightly. I had heard the stories about people dying during the Ironman itself (only one person, but that was enough to make me reflect a little bit). I knew that it would be a huge undertaking and that I couldn't do it without some help along the way. Still, I signed up for the event and there was no turning back. Little did I know, the next nine months would be the most life-changing ever and that finishing the Ironman itself would be just icing on the cake.

Throughout the next months I joined the Landis Triathlon Club, hired a swim coach at Life Time, attended several masters swim classes at ASU, worked with a personal trainer every week and even joined a running/fitness program with a coach of my own.

With swimming by far my weakness, I knew I would struggle desperately if I tried to go it alone. I had done nearly six short distance triathlons before, with the longest swim being only ¾ of a mile. When I started working with my swim coach Hollie at LTF, I still felt like I had to put a gun to my head when I got in the water. I couldn't have done the workouts I needed to do without her. Excuses would have come all too easy, and I hate excuses!

Training for a marathon in and of itself can be a full-time training regimen. I had no idea what was in store for me on the training of three long-distance endurance disciplines.

I trained six days a week and intensified my training with three months to go. I lived at the gym, joking that my new home was Life Time Fitness. I trained sometimes up to three times a day, depending on the day. My business and personal life took a back burner, even at times costing me thousands of dollars in real estate sales because of my devotion to training and understandably my clients having needs that I couldn't always fulfill. Initially that was a hard pill to swallow, but I found that the training was changing me not only physically, but mentally and spiritually, through the dedication and devotion to such a high goal. I felt that the lost money in business would only turn around to come back to me ten-fold in the experience of completing and training for the Ironman.

My friendships evolved and changed during the time as well. No longer could I run every single Saturday morning as I was accustomed to. My running club friendships had to come second after my newfound tri-training Ironman devotees. Saturdays were devoted to lots of time in the saddle (a.k.a. bike seat) and not much other than cycling was done before noon that day. The terms brick (back to back workout combos of two out of the three disciplines), butterfly (swim stroke I learned to strengthen my upper body) and Quintana Roo (brand name of wetsuits) were common every day language for me.

A CLOSE CALL AND FINAL TAPER

"Only those who dare to go too far can possibly find out how far they can go."
- T.S. Elliot

As it got closer to April 9th, I felt an enormous excitement rush over me at every mention of the word Ironman. My stomach would flutter with anticipation. As the countdown went under 90 days, the training was more and more intense and focused. I felt confident that I was going to make it.

With roughly four weeks to go, I made a crucial mistake on one of the last big training weekends that affected my last month of training. I had completed a 15.3-mile run on a Friday morning with Ed, Rob, Karl and Jason (my Life Time buddies), a 1.2-mile swim followed by a 100-mile bikeride and 15-minute jog on Saturday, and a 10K distance race on Sunday. The morning of the race, I felt a twinge in my right foot and didn't think much of it, but the pain came again roughly 3 miles into the run and didn't go away. I wasn't pushing myself beyond a 7-minute/mile pace because I knew I was bordering on some type of injury – I just didn't know how serious it was. I limped back to my car after the finish, praying that I hadn't done too much damage. I would soon learn, however, that I had to spend the next two weeks off of my foot and could only swim and bike. I couldn't believe my stupidity! Lesson #1: Don't flirt with injuries when training for an Ironman – stop when the pain comes.

I received so much support and encouragement from all my friends over that next couple of weeks, and after those long 14 days, I could run pain-free again. With two weeks to go until the big day, I was able to put in a few more miles, but no longer runs – it was taper time. Tapering, in the athletic world of marathons and triathlons can be the most loved or most hated time, depending on the person. It is a gradual diminishing of distance and time training. Typically, the athlete's heaviest training week is the fourth week prior to the race, with the closing three weeks a lot less in distance and time as compared to the previous weeks. The idea is to store up extra energy, get extra rest, damage the body less and be ready to go in top form come race day. Done right, it can be the most valuable time given to training after the most intense part. The body views it as the "calm before the storm". Mentally it can be restful as well, however, some athletes who just start can find it hard to stay away from the training. It becomes a different battle of self-control.

One last chance to build more confidence and test my endurance: I was given the opportunity to do an open-water swim of 2.4 miles, the same distance as the Ironman. I had never swum more than 1.2 miles, so I was excited to see how it would go. I finished it in just 1 hour 28 minutes, and I had hoped for 1 hour 40 minutes! After that we biked 37 miles and I felt great the whole time! I felt as though I could have done the Ironman that day.

But the obstacles to Ironman were not done just yet.

THE FINAL TEST

"I have always believed, and I still believe, that whatever good or bad fortune may come our way we can always give it meaning and transform it into something of value."

-Hermann Hesse

On the Monday before the big day, I was not feeling well. The week before, I had known my immune system was not 100%, so I finally broke down and went to the urgent-care doctor near my office. It was strep throat. I was in shock – I couldn't believe my timing! I had been working toward Ironman for 9 months (or 7 years, to look at it another way) and I was sick. I knew I would have to take antibiotics and then hope and pray that they would do the trick.

I spent that entire week on the couch. No exercise, no working, nothing. I had a lot of time to reflect on the race. What if I didn't get better? What if I couldn't breathe very well? How would a week of doing nothing affect my overall time? Would I even be able to start the race? Would I be able to finish? Why hadn't I listened to my body and rested?

The pastor at my church had just spoken that Sunday about a book entitled "Silence and Solitude", which I purchased on the spot, not knowing that I would have plenty of time to read it After hearing him share about all the type "A" personality traits that push so many of us beyond our human limits and prevent us from taking enough breaks in life, I felt someone was trying to tell me something. My fast-paced life and lack of rest had led me to get sick – and the words in that book were what I needed, and I received them with an open mind and heart during my own deep reflection time of silence and solitude.

That Tuesday, April the 5th also happened to be the seventh anniversary of Mike's death. I spent that day alone, reflecting on really what it was that got me to the Ironman goal – it had all started with Mike. I resolved that no matter what it took, I would at least start the Ironman race for Mike, whether I felt 100% or not. I had come so far and experienced so much – I had to get to that starting line.

Friday morning I tested out my physical energy in my own mini-triathlon. I biked around the block, ran for five minutes and hit the pool for about five minutes of swimming, just to see how my body responded. I was a bit nervous after I got out of the water, but reassured that I wasn't totally drained. Despite the confidence boost, I hit a wall later in the afternoon and had to lay down on the couch, unable to breathe normally and still super-congested.

"Every memorable act in the history of the world is a triumph of enthusiasm. Nothing great was ever achieved without it because it gives any challenge or any occupation, no matter how frightening or difficult, a new meaning. Without enthusiasm you are doomed to a life of mediocrity but with it you can accomplish miracles." -Og Mandino

The morning of the race came quickly. The odd thing was, I didn't feel nervous. I wandered around the transition area, dropping off all my change of clothes bags in the appropriate spots. I shared some excited conversations with many of my training friends and even commiserated with those that were sick as I was. One friend even decided that morning to not compete after feeling dizzy, concerned that he wouldn't make it. I knew how he felt: the uncertainty of what could happen.

The race started as nearly 2000 of us filled Tempe Town Lake, pink and blue caps bobbing up and down, wetsuit clad bodies clamoring past the start line as the cannon shot off at 7 a.m. I took the swim one stroke at a time, focusing on my breathing and how my body felt. I was shocked at how much energy I did feel flowing through me. I only got kicked in the head twice, nearly losing my swim cap at one point. I finished the swim in 1 hour 28 minutes, the exact same time I had recorded when I was healthy. I was so happy. I saw my friend Steve at the wetsuit peeler station and was encouraged to hear many people shouting out my name. Swim accomplished.

I changed into my bike gear and ran to my bike, two volunteers, Jase, my personal trainer, and Micah Thompson, a college friend and biking training partner, checking in with me to make sure I was coherent and okay to move on to the 112-mile ride. They knew the condition I was in was not totally healthy and were concerned. The first few miles were a bit shaky, as I felt a bit unstable and dizzy. I simply slowed down, took in some calories and decided in my mind that this was just going to be an easy training ride – no serious pushing of the limits. I had heard that the wind was gusting above 40 miles per hour, so there was no need to travel at lightning speed anyway.

The course was mostly flat, but the winds did force me to down to nine miles per hour at times. I didn't experience any flat tires (which was a blessing), only had to stop to go to the bathroom once and didn't really feel my body breaking down until mile 85. Then I was counting each mile as it passed.

Tears of joy spilled onto my face when I hit mile 107 and realized I was going to make it! I was overcome with emotion and tried to maintain my composure. As I finished that leg, it felt so good to realize that (funny as it may sound) I only had the marathon leg to go! My bike time was not exactly what I wanted: six hours, 45 minutes. However, I was counting my blessings –there had been no problems mechanically or physically.

I started the marathon at roughly an 8:30 minute-per-mile pace. I felt good. Almost too good. I had fueled my body appropriately on the bike, taking in six Clif bars, a peanut butter sandwich, Fig Newtons, Gatorade, water, and a variety of gu gels. My body was now responding to the run as if I were running a marathon on its own, without having done the two other disciplines. Fortunately, the temperature was a moderate 75 degrees, and the wind was helping keep me cool as well.

My fun, however, ended at mile 15. My physical and emotional energy disappeared and my positive mental attitude was out the window. I couldn't run another step. I swallowed my pride and had to walk. I had never walked in a marathon before, no matter how bad I felt. I was beginning my "death march" to the finish line, and I resigned myself to not finishing in 13 hours, the original goal. I talked myself into believing that this was okay – "I've been sick and on antibiotics the whole week" – but it was just an excuse to allow myself to shut down. I surprised myself with that attitude and was even more surprised that I listened.

"You gain strength, courage, and confidence by each experience in which you really stop to look fear in the face. You are able to say to yourself, 'I have lived through this horror. I can take the next thing that comes

along.' You must do the thing you think you cannot do."

-Eleanor Roosevelt, Former First Lady and Lecturer

With the little resolve I had left, I kept trudging forward, and it wasn't long before two of my triathlete friends shuffled by me. I had just passed them, not long before, at the mile 14 aid station where they had been walking. I felt a twinge of respect, thinking they had overcome their own pain and were running again. They both flashed grins at me and encouraged me to run with them. I was horrified at their suggestion! With every bone in my body screaming "insane," I just muttered that they were crazy and I couldn't do what they were doing. They continued to shuffle/jog by me. Their plan was what mine had been: They were running to each aid station and then walking through the stations for hydration/fueling purposes. That was one mile running and a few paces walking fast.

As their backs faded away toward the next aid station, I felt the taste of disgust in my mouth. Here I am – a runner not running. What was I thinking? It took everything I had, but I managed to suck in a huge breath and let it out in one large sigh. I pushed onward, following my friends ahead, leveraging their moving forms as a dangling carrot in front of me like a hound chasing the hare. I met them at the aid station, stopping when they did, walking stiffly through the place where they loaded us up with water, bananas, oranges and a variety of other refreshments.

I got into a zone and basically focused on each step of each mile, not trying to think of exactly how many miles I had to go to cross the finish line. I pressed on like that, on my own, until Mile 17, where I was greeted for a second time by Steve Elwell (a great friend from Life Time Fitness) at his volunteer aid position. I was not nearly as positive this time around as I had been the first time, and I let him know it. He was not deterred by the lack of positive energy in my voice and he quickly asked me what I needed. I requested water, coke and a couple oranges. His boundless energy and encouragement made me smile, giving me the boost I deserved.

Within seconds I saw Brian Thompson, a triathlete friend who had actually been one reason I signed up for the Ironman Arizona. He had completed an Ironman the year before and signed up for IMAZ immediately, and he told me that with my running background, I could easily finish an Ironman. Now, as we both found each other during our weakest moments of the 140.6-mile race, he encouraged me yet again.

I told him that I had thought I would be able to break 13 hours easily, but now I was doubting myself and resigned to just finishing. Brian is in the mortgage business, so he did the math easily for me. We were 9 miles from the finish and 90 minutes away from breaking 13 hours. All I had to do was average a 10-minute-mile pace for the balance of the race. A new hope was born. I asked Brian to join me for at least a mile to keep us both going and he did agree, though somewhat hesitantly. I knew he wasn't as fond of running as I – he was digging deep to keep going.

We arrived at the next mile marker, mile 18. I grabbed my chicken broth, my newfound love in this endurance event and we walked a few paces slowly but surely. I asked if he was ready to start running again, and he said that he would rather finish walking, given the pain he was in. I knew that I had a difficult task before me. Averaging 10-minute/mile pace is nothing under normal circumstances; however, given the run/walk pattern, I knew that I was barely averaging 10-minute miles, if not worse. The remaining 8 miles would be the most memorable I had ever run.

The sun had set on the Valley, and runners and walkers were doing the Ironman shuffle along the canal path illuminated by big lights that had been brought in so our course would not be completely dark. It was surreal to see the reflective colors on people's silhouettes rather than seeing their full running forms. However, even in the dark, I could see the tiredness and sweat-covered faces as we passed along in the night. I focused on my pace and tried to throw words of encouragement out to those I passed along the final miles – a counterintuitive measure I knew would help me as well.

As I reached mile 23, I looked at my watch to see that it was 7:30 p.m. I had been enduring the course for 12 ½ hours. I had 30 minutes or less to cross that finish line in under 13 hours. 3.2 miles to go. My math skills had returned and I voiced out loud what was in my head. "I have to run faster and take no walking breaks to reach my goal." Only five kilometers were left, and I gave that last stretch everything I had. I was in a zone and no one could stop me. I found a renewed strength and pushed on to a 9-minute/mile pace. I couldn't believe I had that much left in me.

As I cruised along the north side of Tempe Town Lake, I saw my friend Jim Jackson, who had helped me train on some long bike rides. Little did I know, he was calling ahead to let other friends at the finish line know I was on my way. I did not stop once in those last 3.2 miles. I did not want to take any chance of slowing or stopping, in case I wouldn't be able to regain the rhythm and pace I was maintaining.

On the south side of the lake I passed by all the signs posted along the running path by loved ones of other participants, reading "Go mom!", "The Pride Lasts Longer Than The Pain" and other encouraging messages. I read the words and was again thankful that I had something to spur me on. I even shouted more hopeful words to other runners whom I passed, as excited energy crept in my soul when I realized the finish line was less than a mile away.

Under the bridge I saw Jim again. He had biked quickly to catch me one last time before I finished. I flashed him a smile and pushed pass him as the course directed me from the city park we ran through to the final city streets. I recognized many friends cheering me on toward the finish as they stood the darkness scattered amongst the many supporters, spurring me on amongst the crowds of people. I barely missed them as I flashed past them and their faces blurred in the sea if faces and lights. The thought entered my mind, "They have been there since 7 a.m. that morning" and I felt a twinge of gratefulness mixed with emotion.

By this point I had thought the finish line was only a few hundred yards away and I could hear other peoples' names being shouted out as they crossed the finish. However, I knew I wasn't there just yet and the darkness threw me off for a minute as I felt a bit disoriented in following the moving bodies before me around the last circle run from street to street, where the bleachers of people witnessed the finish. I had seen my running coach, Kalombo, Jase and friend Micah and that final boost of encouragement is what propelled me at the finish.

As I rounded that last turn, I couldn't believe I was there. Crossing the finish line was like an out-of-body experience: my official clock time was 12 hours, 57 minutes! Roughly two minutes and change under my 13-hour goal. I was in shock and could only smile a dumb smile as I noticed many familiar friends beyond the finishing tape. The flashing lights and the screaming fans surrounding the finish, in and out of the bleachers, gave an extra boost to the spirit and brought a mixture of emotions to my nearly lifeless body.

The finish line helpers surrounded my body with a Mylar cape to keep my body's warmth from escaping in the cool night air. I saw Dr. Kevin Sherman at the finish after they put an Ironman Arizona finisher's bracelet and medal on me. The medal was heavy and seemed to add more weight to my slowing body, yet I did not care. That medal was a symbol of finishing the biggest event of my life. It could have weighted 10 pounds and I would not have cared. I hugged a few of the other Landis Tri Club friends who were catchers at the finish line and was escorted by a fellow runner who walked me to the fence area where many of my cheering section friends were waiting excitedly to give me hugs.

Much to my surprise, even a couple of realtors from my real estate office had made the trip down to see me finish. Elaine Sans Souci and Mitzie Cordes-Heydt. These two women have been great role models for me in the real estate industry, as well as strong career business owners. I was so moved to have them be by my side as I shuffled around the finishing area. They literally helped me walk by holding me on each side. The shock and disbelief I felt about finishing still engulfed me so much so that I felt as if in a daze and would not remember everything that I said or did those several minutes after finishing. I was deliriously happy.

They escorted me around for the next hour, getting me food, helping pick up all my bags of clothes and leftover food that I didn't use on the course. I had not exactly planned what would happen at the finish line. I don't know what I would have done without them as they even drove me home in my vehicle, offering to take me somewhere to get some food. However, the three pieces of pizza I downed at the finish line was all I needed. Pizza had never tasted so good. The gooey cheese and spicy pepperoni and sausage were not the normal triathlete fare I had experienced the past several months of training. I did not feel guilty this time, however, knowing that I had earned that moment to eat anything I wanted.

As I prepared to leave, many more athletes were still finishing well into the night. I found my bike in the dark sea of bikes in the transition area. Micah also took my bike home for me. Such simple things that I hadn't planned for and everything was taken care of without my even trying. Friends like those are a true blessing.

WHAT I'VE LEARNED

"Life should NOT be a journey to the grave with the intention of arriving safely in an attractive and well preserved body, but rather to skid in sideways, Champagne in one hand - strawberries in the other, body thoroughly used up, totally worn out and screaming WOO HOO - What a Ride!"
-Unknown

The next morning I awoke without an alarm at 5 a.m. – the usual time to train. I smiled to myself as I realized that I did not have to train that day. It was my day of rest, with many more to follow.

As with every major event in life that takes a lot of planning, involved a lot of people, a lot of time and commitment, the day after brought a sense of sadness in my heart. The past nine months of training had culminated in one day, one long event, and I was now an Ironman Triathlete. My first thought was, "What next?"

Without a big goal such as the Ironman I have felt a little lost, but I have also found a new identity and new purpose in my training and my life. I am no longer just a runner. I am a triathlete!

I have learned that swimming actually did help keep my body injury free (as much as I hate to admit it) and well balanced between all the running and biking. I have more aches now since the Ironman with just running than I ever did during the nine months of evolving into a triathlete. Swimming does a body good.

I have learned that swimming kept my body injury-free (as much as I hate to admit it) and well-balanced. I have more aches now, just running, than I ever did during the nine months of evolving into a triathlete. Swimming does a body good.

I've learned that just as in training for an Ironman, so in life – there should be a balance of rest and work when you train. The rest day is just as crucial as the other six of work.

I've learned that we should always try to learn something new to expand our horizons. You never know what you are missing until you try something totally new and challenging.

"The only thing that stands between a man and what he wants from life is often merely the will to try it and the faith to believe that it is possible."
-Richard DeVos

I've learned you never know what your body is capable of doing until you test the limits and go beyond that thresholds that may have held you back before.

I've learned that passion is something that comes from within but is 10 times more meaningful when it is drawn out and shared with others.

I've learned that never giving up on a goal or a dream is what makes you fully realize your potential and your God-given abilities. It makes you wonder, "If I can do this…what is there that I can not do??"

"Look at a day when you are supremely satisfied at the end. It's not a day when you lounge around doing nothing; it's when you've had everything to do, and you've done it."

Margaret Thatcher

I have learned to live in "the now" and not "the next". We are always striving for that next thing, that next race, that next relationship, that next. But there is much more power in "the now" and just enjoying life in the present, taking it all in as it comes, not worrying about tomorrow and what might be or what might have been.

I have learned to listen more and talk less. Listening to my friends as we trained taught me a lot about life and the journey. I was reminded that the words "silent" and "listen" have the same letters, just rearranged.

I have learned that a little silence and solitude and reflection will change the way you see or hear or respond to what goes on around you.

I've learned that we were created for success and that all of us possess a lot of talent and greatness; however, no one succeeds alone. I could not have done the Ironman without all the help along the way. You can possess a lot of internal motivation and go out to train day in and day out all by yourself. But ultimately, the true gifts you have been given will be drawn out by those who are in the arena with you, cheering you on.

I have learned that no one succeeds alone.

FINAL REFLECTIONS

As I have continued my post-Ironman journey, I have learned more about myself every day through my competing and training, and through pursuing my true purpose and meaning in life. Each and every day is an adventure and an important part of the journey. No day is more important than the next and yet each and every one can be wasted entirely by simply not embracing and accepting where you are in that moment. I have learned to love life and love myself and others so much more through my transformational journey.

Wherever you may be in life, I wish you much success on your journey and I pray you surround yourself with a lot of great people to help you reach your goals and achieve your dreams along the way. That's what life is all about!

"When you give someone a book, you don't give him just paper, ink, and glue. You give him the possibility of a whole new life."

-Christopher Morley

One last note. If this book inspired you in any way, please let me know and please pass it on. I would love to hear your story and share mine with your friends and family. Please pass this book on or find out how to order more at my website www.transformationtrisystems.com. Feel free to contact me at 480-570-7653 or Lois@TransformedTriathlete.com